# ZEPHANIAH, NAHUM, AND HABAKKUK

# CASCADE COMPANIONS

The Christian theological tradition provides an embarrassment of riches: from Scripture to modern scholarship, we are blessed with a vast and complex theological inheritance. And yet this feast of traditional riches is too frequently inaccessible to the general reader.

The Cascade Companions series addresses the challenge by publishing books that combine academic rigor with broad appeal and readability. They aim to introduce nonspecialist readers to that vital storehouse of authors, documents, themes, histories, arguments, and movements that comprise this heritage with brief yet compelling volumes.

RECENT TITLES IN THIS SERIES:

*Cascade Companion to Evil* by Charles Taliaferro
*Metaphysics* by Donald Wallenfang
*Phenomenology* by Donald Wallenfang
*Virtue* by Olli-Pekka Vainio
*Reading Paul* by Michael Gorman
*The Rule of Faith* by Everett Ferguson
*The Second-Century Apologists* by Alvyn Pettersen
*Origen* by Ronald E. Heine
*Athanasius of Alexandria* by Lois Farag
*Practicing Lament* by Rebekah Eklund
*Forgiveness: A Theology* by Anthony Bash
*Called to Attraction: The Theology of Beauty* by Brendan T. Sammon
*A Primer in Ecotheology* by Celia Deane-Drummond
*Postmodern Theology* by Carl Raschke
*Jacques Ellul* by Jacob E. Van Vleet and Jacob M. Rollinson
*Understanding Pannenberg* by Anthony C. Thiselton
*The Becoming of God: Process Theology* by Ronald Faber
*Theology and Science Fiction* by James F. McGrath
*The U.S. Immigration Crisis* by Miguel de la Torre
*Feminism and Christianity* by Caryn Riswold
*Queer Theology* by Linn Marie Tonstad

# ZEPHANIAH, NAHUM, AND HABAKKUK

*Hebrew Prophets
of the Seventh Century*

JACK R. LUNDBOM

CASCADE *Books* • Eugene, Oregon

ZEPHANIAH, NAHUM, AND HABAKKUK
Hebrew Prophets of the Seventh Century

Cascade Companions

Copyright © 2025 Jack R. Lundbom. All rights reserved. Except for brief quotations in critical publications or reviews, no part of this book may be reproduced in any manner without prior written permission from the publisher. Write: Permissions, Wipf and Stock Publishers, 199 W. 8th Ave., Suite 3, Eugene, OR 97401.

Cascade Books
An Imprint of Wipf and Stock Publishers
199 W. 8th Ave., Suite 3
Eugene, OR 97401

www.wipfandstock.com

PAPERBACK ISBN: 979-8-3852-0580-6
HARDCOVER ISBN: 979-8-3852-0581-3
EBOOK ISBN: 979-8-3852-0582-0

*Cataloguing-in-Publication data:*

Names: Lundbom, Jack R., author.
Title: Zephaniah, Nahum, and Habakkuk : Hebrew prophets of the seventh century / Jack R. Lundbom.
Description: Eugene, OR: Cascade Books, 2025. | Includes bibliographical references and indexes.
Identifiers: ISBN 979-8-3852-0580-6 (paperback). | ISBN 979-8-3852-0581-3 (hardcover). | ISBN 979-8-3852-0582-0 (ebook).
Subjects: LSCH: Bible. Zephaniah—Criticism, interpretation, etc. | Bible. Nahum—Criticism, interpretation, etc. | Bible. Habakkuk—Criticism, interpretation, etc.
Classification: BS1560.5 L86 2025 (print). | BS1560 (ebook).

VERSION NUMBER 01/16/25

Scripture quotations marked (KJV) are from the Authorized Version (1611), which is in the public domain.

Scripture quotations marked (NJB) are from the New Jerusalem Bible © 1985 by Daron, Longman and Todd, Doubleday, and Cerf. All rights reserved.

Scripture quotations marked (NRSV) are taken from the New Revised Standard Version Bible © 1989 by the Division of Christian Education of the National Council of the Churches of Christ in the United States of America. Used by permission. All rights reserved.

Scripture quotations marked (NJPS) are from *Tanakh: The New JPS Translation According to the Traditional Hebrew Text*. Copyright © 1985, 1999 by The Jewish Publication Society with the permission of the publisher.

Scripture quotations marked (RSV) are taken from the Revised Standard Version Bible © 1946, 1952, 1971 by the Division of Christian Education of the National Council of the Churches of Christ in the United States of America. Used by permission. All rights reserved.

*To*
*Douglas W. Johnson*
*Preacher, Pastor, and Churchman*

# CONTENTS

*Preface* | xi
*Abbreviations* | xiii

1  Judah in the Seventh Century | 1
2  Prophets of the Seventh Century | 10

## ZEPHANIAH

3  "The Day of Yahweh Is at Hand" (1:2–18) | 45
4  "Seek Yahweh, You Humble of the Land" (2:1–15) | 57
5  "Woe to the Defiant, Defiled, and Oppressing City" (3:1–7) | 65
6  "Therefore Wait for Me, Oracle of Yahweh" (3:8–20) | 70

## NAHUM

7  "Yahweh Is Taking Vengeance on His Adversaries" (1:2–11) | 79
8  "I Will Break Its Yoke-bar from Upon You" (1:12–14) | 86
9  "Look Upon the Mountains: One Who Brings Good Tidings!" (1:15—2:13 [Heb 2:1–14]) | 89
10  "Woe to the Bloody City!" (3:1–19) | 97

## HABAKKUK

11  "A Work Is Being Done in Your Days" (1:2–17) | 109
12  "The Righteous Will Live by His Faithfulness" (2:1–5) | 115

*Contents*

13 "But Yahweh Is in His Holy Temple" (2:6b–20) | 120

14 "Yahweh the Lord Is My Strength" (3:2–19) | 128

*Bibliography* | 137

*Name Index* | 141

*Scripture Index* | 143

# PREFACE

THIS BOOK SEEKS TO put before the general reader the background and preaching of three Hebrew prophets active in the late seventh century: Zephaniah, Nahum, and Habakkuk—all contemporaries of better-known Jeremiah. Like other books in the Cascade Companion series, it limits technical discussion and footnotes, leaving readers to consult larger commentaries and works cited in the bibliography.

While the prophecies and actions of all three prophets are not generally well known, each has nevertheless left his mark on the collective memory of the community of faith. Zephaniah is remembered for his "Day of the Lord" prophecy, also for saying he will search Jerusalem with a lamp to seek out evidoers. Habakkuk is the one who said "the righteous shall live by his faith(fulness), which became so important for the apostle Paul in writing to the church at Rome; also for saying, "The LORD is in his holy temple, let all the earth keep silent before him," which has become widely used in Christian liturgy and worship. Nahum, for his part, is the only voice in the entire Old Testament to prophesy and celebrate the falling of a much-hated Assyrian empire in 612.

I am dedicating this book to my good friend the Reverend Douglas W. Johnson, retired minister of the Evangelical

Covenant Church. Doug has been an outstanding preacher, faithful to the great truths of Scripture and at the same time well-attuned to issues great and small in the world around us. He is an avid reader of the Hebrew prophets, listening not only to voices of the better-known Isaiah and Jeremiah, but also to voices of the so-called Minor Prophets of the Old Testament.

Scripture translations in the book, except as otherwise noted, are my own.

Jack R. Lundbom<br>
Kennebunk, Maine<br>
March 9, 2024

# ABBREVIATIONS

| | |
|---|---|
| AB | The Anchor Bible |
| ABD | *The Anchor Bible Dictionary*. Edited by David Noel Freedman. New York: Doubleday, 1992 |
| ANE | Ancient Near East(ern) |
| ANEP² | *The Ancient Near East in Pictures*. 2nd ed. with Supplement. Edited by James B. Pritchard. Princeton: Princeton University Press, 1969 |
| ANET³ | *Ancient Near Eastern Texts Relating to the Old Testament*. 3rd ed. with Supplement. Edited by James B. Pritchard. Princeton: Princeton University Press, 1969 |
| *Ant.* | *Jewish Antiquities*, by Flavius Josephus. Translated by Ralph Marcus. Cambridge: Harvard University Press, 1966 |
| Ar | Arabic |
| AramB | The Aramaic Bible |
| BHQ | *Biblia Hebraica Quinta: The Twelve Minor Prophets*. Edited by Anthony Gelston. Stuttgart, 2010 |
| BM | British Museum |
| CBQ | *Catholic Biblical Quarterly* |

| | |
|---|---|
| *CovH* | *The Hymnal of the Evangelical Covenant Church of America.* Chicago: Covenant Press, 1950 |
| Eng | English |
| Gk | Greek |
| GKC | *Gesenius' Hebrew Grammar.* 2nd ed. Edited by E. Kautzch. Translated by A. E. Cowley. Oxford: Clarendon, 1963 |
| Heb | Hebrew |
| ICC | International Critical Commentary |
| *Int* | *Interpretation* |
| *JSS* | *Journal of Semitic Studies* |
| KJV | Authorized King James Version of the Bible (1611) |
| LCL | Loeb Classical Library |
| lit. | literally |
| LXX | The Greek Septuagint according to *Septuaginta II.* 18th ed. Edited by Alfred Rahlfs. Stuttgart: Deutsche Bibelgesellschaft, 1965 |
| $M^L$ | Massoretic Text according to the Leningrad Codex B19A |
| MT | The Massoretic Text of the Hebrew Bible according to *BHQ.* Edited by Anthony Gelston. Stuttgart: Deutsche Bibelgesellschaft, 2010 |
| NJB | New Jerusalem Bible |
| NJPS | *Tanakh: The New JPS Translation According to the Traditional Hebrew Text* |
| NRSV | New Revised Standard Version |
| OTL | Old Testament Library |
| 1QpHab | Qumran fragment of Habakkuk in *Biblia Qumranica 3B: Minor Prophets.* Edited by Beate Ego et al. Leiden: Brill, 2005 |

| | |
|---|---|
| 4QpNah | Qumran fragment of Nahum in *Biblia Qumranica 3B: Minor Prophets*. Edited by Beate Ego et al. Leiden: Brill, 2005 |
| RSV | Revised Standard Version |
| *Tg* | *The Targum of the Minor Prophets*. AramB 14. Edited by Kevin J. Cathcart and Robert P. Gordon. Wilmington, DE: Glazier, 1989 |
| VTSup | Supplements to Vetus Testamentum |
| *ZAW* | *Zeitschrift für die alttestamentliche Wissenschaft* |

1

# JUDAH IN THE SEVENTH CENTURY

THE SEVENTH CENTURY SAW Assyria still the major power-broker in the ANE. It would continue to be so for the greater part of the century, until the death of Assurbanipal in 627 and the nation's demise a few years later. Its history merits description in some detail. It is hard to overestimate the impact Assyria had on neighboring nations, its hand falling heavily upon Northern Israel and Judah with disastrous results. Assyria was a brutal nation. Religious practices imported into Judah during the reigns of Ahaz and Manasseh led Zephaniah and Jeremiah to prophesy uncompromising judgment on Yahweh's covenant people, and these practices also explain Nahum's unconcealed joy at Nineveh being destroyed in 612.

## THE RISE OF ASSYRIA

Assyria's rise as a formidable world power began with Tiglath-pileser III (745–727). Northern Israel had been strong under the long reign of Jeroboam II (786–746), and Judah was similarly strong during the long reign of Uzziah/Azariah (783–742), but after the death of both kings things would change dramatically, especially in Northern Israel where, led by an unblessed succession of weak and incompetent kings, the nation tottered and spiraled to an inglorious defeat.

In 743 Tiglath-pileser made campaigns into Syria, and a decade later overran Galilee and Transjordan, taking Israelite people into faraway exile (2 Kgs 15:29; cf. *ANET*[3] 282–84). Hazor and Megiddo were destroyed, and Megiddo became an Assyrian provincial capital. Tiglath took Damascus in 732, and from there went south to conquer the Chaldeans, taking the Babylonian throne in 729. He campaigned also against the Medes in what is now northern Iran.

The next Assyrian king, Shalmaneser V (726–722), attacked Northern Israel in 724. Samaria, which had no natural water supply, held out for two years, but in 722 Shalmaneser took the city and his successor, Sargon II (721–705), carried away those remaining to Assyria and to the cities of the Medes (2 Kgs 17:3–6). He also brought peoples from Babylon and other eastern cities to populate a rebuilt Samaria and surrounding cities, making it another Assyrian province (2 Kgs 17:24; *ANET*[3] 284–85). We meet these peoples later as the Samaritans.

Judah was now all that remained of a truncated Israelite state. King Ahaz (735–15) remained an Assyrian vassal throughout his reign, but because Sargon faced rebellions in Babylon and elsewhere, and because Egypt at the time was reasserting itself, Sargon made no campaigns into Judah after 720. The reign of Ahaz was remembered as one of great apostasy (2 Kings 16). The prophet Isaiah, having no influence with Ahaz, went into retirement (Isa 8:16–17). But his prophecies of a good king the likes of David (e.g., Isa 9:2–7; 11:1–9) would loom large in Israel's later messianic hope.

Judah's next king Hezekiah (715–687) sought to free Judah from its harsh Assyrian yoke, and for a brief period he would enjoy a measure of success. But it would not last long. Sometime between 712–11 Hezekiah undertook a major reform (2 Kgs 18:3–6; 2 Chr 29–31). Isaiah, now emerged from retirement, enjoyed good relations with Hezekiah and had considerable influence with him. The prophet Micah also had a good influence upon Hezekiah (Jer 26:17–19). Sargon apparently did nothing to interfere, being occupied with rebellions elsewhere, and his successor Sennacherib (704–681) at first did nothing. But then Hezekiah withheld tribute from Sennacherib (2 Kgs 18:7), which brought the Assyrian king and his army into Judah in 701.

## ASSYRIAN DOMINATION IN THE SEVENTH CENTURY

Sennacherib in his records says he destroyed 46 fortified Judahite cities and countless unwalled villages, leaving Hezekiah in Jerusalem "like a bird in a cage" (*ANET*³ 287–88; cf. 2 Kgs 18:13). According to the biblical record Sennacherib at first put Hezekiah under heavy tribute, but then Hezekiah held out. The city was miraculously spared, and sometime after returning home Sennacherib was assassinated by two of his sons. Esarhaddon, another son, took the throne (2 Kgs 19:35–37; *ANET*³ 289–90).[1] Events after

---

1. The history here is less than certain, in part because of a suspected telescoping of events in the biblical record. John Bright supports a two-campaign theory of Sennacherib, the first in 701 resulting in Hezekiah's surrender and paying the Assyrian king a hefty tribute. When Sennacherib came a second time in 689, Hezekiah held out and Jerusalem was spared by the miraculous deliverance. The king both times was supported by the prophet Isaiah.

701 are uncertain. We have no extra-biblical records on the last years of Sennacherib. According to a lower chronology, Esarhaddon is believed to have ruled from 680–669. After assuming the throne he turned his attention to Egypt and countries west of the Euphrates, one of which was Judah (*ANET*[3] 290–94).

The reign of Hezekiah in Judah had been a relatively good one, but Manasseh (687–642), who succeeded him, dismantled the reforms, and pagan religious practices again flourished openly. Manasseh's reign was a return to the rule of Ahaz, a time characterized by a syncretism in which the religion of Yahweh was combined with Assyrian religion and Baal religion of Canaan. Against Baal Yahweh was believed to be powerless to act (Zeph 1:12). Throughout Manasseh's reign Judah was subservient politically and religiously to its Assyrian overlords, who after Sennacherib were Esarhaddon and Assurbanipal (668–627). Judah would remain subservient for over forty years. Biblical writers express outrage at what went on during this time and, except for the Chronicler, were unforgiving of Manasseh (2 Kgs 21:1–21; 23:26; 24:3–4; Jer 15:4; cf. 2 Chr 33:10–20). No prophets are known to have arisen during Manasseh's reign, but prophets who came later bore ample witness to the ruinous effect this king had upon Judah (Zeph 1:8; Jer 15:4).

## THE REFORM OF JOSIAH

Manasseh's long reign came to an end in 642. Amon became king and sought to continue his father's policies, but two years later was assassinated by an anti-Assyrian party. Those responsible were punished since Assyrian reprisal was feared (2 Kgs 21:23–24). Assurbanipal was still on the throne in Nineveh.

A ray of hope nevertheless dawned in Judah with the ascent of Josiah to the Jerusalem throne in 640. He was a lad of only eight years, and leading citizens in Jerusalem now wanted a change in how the ship of state was guided. The next three decades saw Judah gradually regain political and religious independence. Prophetic voices were again heard, and Judah experienced a major reform. The long subservience to Assyria appeared to end.

The reform, according to the Chronicler, began in Josiah's twelfth year, which was 628 (2 Chr 34:3b)[2], with a purge of idolatrous worship in and around Jerusalem. Josiah pulled down worship sites to Baal and demolished incense altars to Baal. Sacred poles, carved and cast images, were broken down. Bones of idolatrous priests were burned on their altars. Jerusalem and all the towns of Judah were purged of Baal worship. The purge of worship sites then went south into the old territory of Simeon (Beersheba), and northward into the Assyrian provinces of Samaria, Gilead, and Galilee (2 Chr 34:3b–7).

The account in 2 Kings, which places the purge later than Chronicles does, provides more detail. The Temple was cleansed of vessels made for Baal, Asherah, and the host of heaven, after which they were burned in the Valley of Kidron. Idolatrous priests in Jerusalem and other cities of Judah were deposed, and high places from Geba to Beersheba were defiled. The high place and altar at Bethel was pulled down, and other idolatrous places were desecrated north and south. Mediums and wizards were also put away (2 Kgs 23:4–20, 24).

In 622, in the midst of repairs being made to the Temple, a lawbook of Moses was found. When read to the king he tore his clothes in shock and remorse (2 Kgs 22:3–13; 2 Chr 34:8–21). A prophetess, Huldah, residing

2. Lundbom, "Lawbook of the Josianic Reform," 294–95.

in Jerusalem's Second Quarter, was consulted by Hilkiah the priest, Shaphan the scribe, and others, and after hearing words on the scroll, Huldah gave the bad and good news. Disaster would come upon the place, but because Josiah had torn his clothes and humbled himself he would be spared the disaster and die in peace (2 Kgs 22:14–20; 2 Chr 34:22–28). The king made a covenant to follow Yahweh and his commandments, with people joining in, and a grand passover, described in greater detail by the Chronicler, was celebrated (2 Chr 35:1–19; 2 Kgs 23:1–3, 21–23).

## THE FALL OF ASSYRIA

In 640 Assurbanipal had regained a measure of control over his empire, which for fifteen years or more had been in rebellion. The Assyrian king, by his own admission, was ambitious and successful, claiming even to have been able to read and write (*ANET*³ 294–301). We know little of the king's activities after 640, only that his years were peaceful enough for him to act as a patron of literature and the arts. British archaeologists in the 1850s came upon his huge library at Nineveh, yielding a treasure of cuneiform texts that are now housed in the basement of the British Museum.

Momentous changes, however, were taking place on the international scene. At the time of Assurbanipal's death, which can be dated by the Haran Inscription to 627 (*ANET*³ 560–562), the once mighty empire of Assyria was fast breaking up.[3] Babylon to the south was in open revolt, as is known from the Babylonian Chronicle, and in October 626 Nabopolassar (626–25) defeated an Assyrian army outside the city of Babylon. A month later he declared himself King of Babylon. The Medes had also become strong, attacking Nineveh after Assurbabipal's death but being beaten off

3. Brinkman, *Prelude to Empire*, 108–10.

with help from the Scythians.[4] Under Cyaxarus (625–585) the Medes were again ready to attack Nineveh and destroy the city.[5] Egypt, Judah, and other states in Palestine and Syria had gained their independence. Assyria was on the defensive, and in less than twenty years would be no more.

Nineveh fell in 612 after a three-month siege to a coalition of Babylonians and the Medes. Two years later the allies dislodged an Assyrian refuge government in Haran. In 609 Egypt came to Assyria's aid in an attempt to retake Haran, but the mission failed. Josiah had gone north to try and stop Neco II, but was slain by the Pharaoh at Megiddo (2 Kgs 23:29–30; 2 Chr 35:20–24). Babylon was now the new power-broker in the ANE.

## JUDAH TOTTERING UNDER KING JEHOIAKIM

As the seventh century drew to a close Judah was on the verge of collapse. Neco, after returning from his unsuccessful errand to the north, took charge of things in Jerusalem. The young Jehoahaz, who had been made king, was deposed and taken to Egypt. His older brother, Eliakim, whose regnal name became Jehoiakim, was placed on the throne. The nation was put under heavy tribute and for the next four years was under Egyptian domination. Independence had ended, the reform was over, and Jehoiakim was beholden to the Pharaoh of Egypt. But a new threat loomed on the horizon.

Egyptian and Babylonian armies were fighting on the north Euphrates. In 605 Nebuchadnezzar II, who was now directing the army in the field, made a surprise attack on the Egyptians at Carchemish, roundly defeating them (Jer 46:2). The Babylonians were now in control of all Mesopotamia. At

4. *Herodotus I*, 102.
5. *Herodotus I*, 103.

the end of 604 Nebuchadnezzar was in the Philistine Plain, where he proceeded to destroy Ashkelon (Jeremiah 47). Jehoiakim proclaimed a fast in Jerusalem (Jer 36:9), doubtless in response to this threat. He also transferred his allegiance to Babylon (2 Kgs 24:1), and for three years became Nebuchadnezzar's vassal. The next year Nebuchadnezzar destroyed Ekron (Tel Miqne). Then in 601 Jehoiakim declared independence from Babylon, which he lived to regret.

In December 598, Nebuchadnezzar came with the Babylonian army to Jerusalem, bringing the city to its knees. Jehoiakim's rule had been a disaster, and Jeremiah predicted for him a violent death (Jer 22:18–19). The beaten king was likely assassinated. The Bible remains silent about his end, except to say that "he slept with his fathers" (2 Kgs 24:6). Jehoiachin, his eighteen-year old son, was put on the throne. Three months later, in March 597, Jerusalem surrendered to Nebuchadnezzar. Jehoiachin, the queen mother, high government officials, and Jerusalem's most skilled workers were deported to Babylon (2 Kgs 24:10–16; Jer 29:2). Nebuchadnezzar placed Zedekiah on the throne (2 Kgs 24:17). In little more than a decade Nebuchadnezzar returned to destroy Jerusalem and all Judah. Yahweh's covenant people thus came to an inglorious end, but unlike the Assyrians and later Babylonians, a remnant would survive to see a better day.

## REFLECTION

1. Do any nations in the modern world appear as brutal as Assyria was? If so, name some.

2. When the Assyrian nation was brought down by the Babylonians and Medes in 612, it came to an end, never to rise again. Why do you think the United

States set up the Marshall Plan to rebuild Germany and Europe after World War II? Why did general Douglas MacArthur, that great maker of peace, seek to rebuild Japan at the end of World War II? And why did President George H. W. Bush act kindly toward Mikhail Gorbachev and Russia when the Soviet Union broke up in the early 1990s?

3. Nebuchadnezzar brought Assyria and other nations to an end. He also destroyed Jerusalem and what remained of the Israelite nation. Why do you think Israel lived to see a new day under the Persians in 539, and become a state once again in 1948?

4. Jehoiakim's rule had been a disaster. Was Judah's fall inevitable, or could the king have done something to prevent the events of 598–597?

# 2

# PROPHETS OF THE SEVENTH CENTURY

## THE TWELVE PROPHETS

TWELVE PROPHETS ARE REFERRED to in Sir 49:10 where it says they comforted the people and gave them hope. These prophets in the Hebrew Bible are Hosea, Joel, Amos, Obadiah, Jonah, Micah, Nahum, Habakkuk, Zephaniah, Haggai, Zechariah, and Malachi, whose prophecies were probably combined on a single scroll at the time Sirach was written, i.e., ca. 180. The collection has also been called "The Minor Prophets," a title first appearing in Augustine.[1] Augustine referred to the small size of these works when compared with the collected works of Isaiah, Jeremiah, and Ezekiel, who were "The Major Prophets."

---

1. Augustine, *De civitate dei* xviii, 29; cf. Eissfeldt, *Old Testament*, 383.

## WHAT MANNER OF INDIVIDUAL IS THE PROPHET?

### Love of Kindness

Abraham Heschel in his great work probing the mind and inner feelings of the prophets[2] says that prophets show a love of kindness, citing Zephaniah as an example:

> The demand is not only to respect justice in the sense of abstaining from doing injustice, but also to strive for it, to pursue it:
> *Seek the LORD, all you humble of the land,*
> *who do his commands;*
> *seek righteousness, seek humility;*
> *perhaps you may be hidden*
> *on the day of the anger of the Lord.*
>     (Zeph 2:3)

### On Divine Anger

Abraham Heschel says the following about divine anger:[3]

> In the numerous biblical statements about the attributes of God, the adjectives used are "good," "righteous," "merciful," "gracious." Only once does the expression "angry [or wrathful] God" occur. (Nah 1:2)

However, he says:[4]

> It is impossible to understand the meaning of divine anger without pondering the meaning of *divine patience* or forbearance. Explicitly and implicitly, the prophets stress that God is patient, long-suffering, or slow to anger (*'erekh appayim*).

---

2. Heschel, *Prophets*, 207.
3. Heschel, *Prophets*, 291.
4. Heschel, *Prophets*, 285.

Nah 1:3 is quoted along with other texts from the Prophets; Exod 34:6; Num 14:18; and the Psalms. Heschel discerns an "embarrassment of anger" in the prophets, again citing Nahum:[5]

> The prophets, we are told, spoke of a God who stands for all the virtues we should like to see in human beings. The harsh words, the grave threats, the relentless demands, the shrieks of doom, are usually disregarded. There are hurricanes in the world as well as lilies. The prophets preached justice and celebrated God's eternal love. But they also proclaimed the danger of man's presumption, the scandal of idolatry and human ruthlessness, and above all the seriousness of divine wrath.
>
> *Who can stand before His indignation?*
> *Who can endure His anger?*
> *His wrath is poured out like fire,*
> *The rocks are broken asunder by Him*
>     (Nah 1:6)

## On Divine Mercy

Heschel says that with divine anger also goes divine mercy, with Habakkuk's psalm in chapter three cited as an example:[6]

> God's concern is the prerequisite and source of His anger. It is because He cares for man that His anger may be kindled against man. Anger and mercy are not opposites, but correlatives. Thus Habakkuk prays: "In wrath remember mercy"
>     (Hab 3:2)

---

5. Heschel, *Prophets*, 279.
6. Heschel, *Prophets*, 283.

## On Seeking the Highest Good

Heschel says prophets seek the highest good, again citing Habakkuk:[7]

> Those who have a sense of beauty know that a stone sculptured by an artist's poetic hands has an air of loveliness; that a beam charmingly placed utters a song. The prophet's ear, however, is attuned to a cry imperceptible to others. A clean house or a city architecturally distinguished may yet fill the prophet with distress:
>> *Woe to him who heaps up what is not his own, ...*
>> *Woe to him who gets evil gain for his house, ...*
>> *For the stone cries out from the wall,*
>> *And the beam from the woodwork responds.*
>> *Woe to him who builds a town with blood,*
>> *And founds a city on iniquity!*
>>    (Hab 2:6, 9, 11–12)

## ZEPHANIAH

The superscription to the book of Zephaniah says that the prophet was the son of Cush, the son of Gedaliah, the son of Amariah, the son of Hezekiah (Zeph 1:1). Since his genealogy is traced back four generations, Hezekiah must be King Hezekiah of Judah. Zephaniah would then have royal blood, something highly unusual for a Hebrew prophet. Zephaniah is said to have prophesied during the days of King Josiah of Judah (i.e., 640–609), which would make him a contemporary of Jeremiah, probably an early contemporary. Zephaniah would then be the first known prophetic voice to be heard in Judah since Isaiah, i.e., since 701.

7. Heschel, *Prophets*, 7.

Hezekiah was remembered as a good king, "doing what was right in the sight of Yahweh just as his ancestor David had done" (2 Kgs 18:3). He rooted out pagan worship and upheld Yahweh's commandments given through Moses, and Yahweh was said to be with him (2 Kgs 18:4–7). Hezekiah had good relations with the prophet Isaiah, whose divine word saved the good king and Jerusalem when Sennacherib attacked the city in 701, and could have brought Israelite nationhood to an end. Zephaniah in his prophetic ideals follows largely in the footsteps of Isaiah. Driver says:

> With Zephaniah, as with Isaiah, the central idea is that of a *judgment*, to be executed by Yahweh upon Judah, which will sweep away from it the idolaters, the men of violence and wrong, judges and others in high position who forget their responsibilities, false prophets and profane priests, the hardened men of the world who have no religion at all ("the men that are thickened upon their lees," i. 12), and who think that Yahweh can do "neither good nor evil," and the impenitent who will not listen to "correction" (i. 4–6, 8f., 12, iii. 2, 3f., 11); but which will leave behind a meek and pious "remnant," who trust simply in their God, and do their duty in every way to their neighbors (ii. 3, iii. 12, 13), who have no longer anything to fear from their ancient enemies (ii. 4–15), but live a life of peace and felicity under Yahweh's immediate kingship (ii. 7, iii. 14–17). This is, in general, the doctrine of Isaiah (i. 25–27, iv. 3–6, xxviii. 5f., xxx. 19–26, 27–33, xxxi. 8f., xxxii. 16–19; cf. on Zeph. iii. 11).[8]

If Zephaniah began preaching in Josiah's twelfth year (628), which according to the Chronicler was the beginning of the reform (2 Chr 34:3b), he anticipated the finding of

---

8. Driver, *Minor Prophets*, 106.

the temple lawbook and major events of 622 (2 Kgs 22:3—23:3, 21–23), and would have been an older contemporary of Jeremiah. He could also be credited with pushing for reform. But Zephaniah also anticipates the fall of Assyria in 612 (Zeph 2:13–15), which means he could have been active also in the latter days of Josiah.

Zephaniah's first prophecy in 1:2–18 is on a coming Day when Yahweh will sweep away everything in creation, but more specifically inhabitants of Judah and Jerusalem who are wicked and devoted to Baal and other forms of idolatrous worship. Leading citizens will be invited guests to a sacrifice in which they will be the victims; Judah's enemies will also be in attendance. On this day howlings will be heard in every quarter of Jerusalem and on the surrounding hills, with people right and left being cut off.

Zephaniah will search the dark corners of Jerusalem with a lamp, seeking out those who believe Yahweh will do neither good nor evil. But it is the idols who do neither good nor evil (cf. Jer 10:5). These and others will become plunder for their enemies. The great day of Yahweh is then described in more detail. It will be one of distress; of ruin and destruction; of darkness and gloom; of thick clouds, trumpet blasts, and cries of those forced into battle. All this will come about because people have sinned against Yahweh. Nothing will be able to save them on the terrible day of Yahweh's wrath.

Zephaniah's second prophecy is a call for Jerusalem to repent and seek Yahweh before it is too late (2:1–4). They are duly warned because judgment is coming on four cities of the Philistines. This warning is followed by a prophecy against the nations and their gods, beginning with the Philistines and ending climactically with Ashur and Nineveh in Assyria (2:5–15).

Zephaniah's third prophecy declares woe upon the defiant, defiled city of Jerusalem, filled as it is with oppression (3:1–7). She listens to no one, takes no correction, and puts no trust in Yahweh. Officials, judges, prophets, and priests are all unworthy of their office, given only to exploiting the poor and less fortunate. Yahweh, by contrast, does no wrong. Morning by morning his justice shines forth. Yahweh has therefore cut off the nations; their battlements are in ruins and no one is walking their streets. He had hoped that his own people would revere him, but it was a vain hope. Instead they rise early only to do corrupt deeds.

Zephaniah's fourth prophecy calls upon people to wait for Yahweh because he intends to address the prey, viz., his oppressed covenant people, and gather nations to pour out his judgment upon them. He will then turn speech of the nations into a pure speech so all will abandon their praying and swearing to other gods, and call upon his name and serve him only. From distant lands exiles will return home bearing offerings in procession.

In that day Judah will not be shamed as in days past, for Yahweh will remove the proud and haughty so they will no longer be found on Zion, Yahweh's holy mountain. Yahweh will leave in Judah's midst a people humble and lowly, who seek refuge in his name. They will do no wrong and speak no lies. Yahweh will make them lie down as sheep in a peaceful pasture where none will make them afraid.

The concluding verses of the prophecy have both the prophet and Yahweh singing with joy over the coming days, for Yahweh has commuted Judah's sentence. Yahweh is the "Warrior" who brings salvation. He will rejoice over his people with joy and quietly renew them in his love. He will also deal with those for whom reproach has been a burden. His people he will make a praise and a name.

## NAHUM

From the superscription to the collection of Nahum's prophecies we learn only that this prophet came from an unknown place called Elkosh and that his oracle concerned Nineveh (1:1). Since Nahum rejoiced with Judah at the renewed celebration of pilgrim feasts once Nineveh had fallen (1:15), he probably came from somewhere in Judah and did his preaching in Jerusalem. The whole of his prophecy describes the capture, sacking, and jubilation over Nineveh's fall, and with it the demise of the Assyrian empire. Nahum's prophecies must be dated ca. 612 when Nineveh was destroyed by the Babylonians and Medes. A date prior to or during the destruction seems preferable. Robert's date between 640 and 630, while not impossible, is too early.

Nahum first prophecy in 1:2–11 begins by affirming Yahweh as a jealous and avenging God, especially against enemies, one who will by no means acquit the guilty. The prophet goes on to describe the effect of Israel's God upon the natural order, noting that his wrath is poured out like fire. Yahweh is good to those who seek refuge in him, but of his enemies he will make a full end. Why then does Nineveh plot against Yahweh?

What follows is a divine oracle (1:12–14) telling Judahites that while Yahweh afflicted them in the past he will do so no longer. The enemy will be cut off. Yahweh will break the yoke-bar and straps Assyria's king has long held over the covenant people. Then turning to address Assyria, Yahweh says he will cut off its carved and molten images and make a grave for Nineveh, for it is of small account.

Nahum's third prophecy (1:15—2:13), which is the heart of his message, describes in vivid detail the capture and sack of Nineveh. But before offering this description, the prophet reports the welcome sight of a messenger coming over the mountains bringing Judah news of peace. The worthless intruder will pass through Judah no longer; it has been utterly cut off, and Judah can once again celebrate her pilgrim festivals and pay her vows.

The prophet then turns to address the Assyrian king, telling him that a "scatterer" has come up against him. Preparations are ironically advised. Ramparts must be guarded and all roads must be watched. Nineveh's defenders must be courageous in battle. Yahweh is nevertheless acting to bring back Israel's former pride even though this enemy ravaged it in days past.

Attacking soldiers hold shields of blood red and are seen to be smartly dressed, their chariots rush madly in suburban streets and squares. The king remembers his commanders, but they stumble as they take up the march. The enemy hastens to the city wall and sets up a mantelet. River gates are opened; the palace is dissolved in a flood of water, and attackers pour into the city. Then the inevitable happens: one of Nineveh's royalty is captured, stripped of her clothing, and carried away. Her maidens moan, beating their breasts. The population is in disarray; treasures are greedily seized by the attackers. Nahum then taunts Assyria, asking where now lies the den of this once-fearless lion who walked with his lioness and cubs unmolested, and filled its den with torn flesh?

The present prophecy ends with a word from Yahweh. He is against Nineveh; he will burn its chariots with fire and its young will be victims of the sword. Yahweh will cut off prey taken from everywhere, and no longer will the voice of Nineveh's messengers be heard among the nations.

Nahum's final prophecy (3:1–19) is a woe upon bloody Nineveh, full of deceit, booty, and prey beyond counting. The attack on the city is developed further: galloping horses, leaping chariots, and no end to dead bodies. Destruction has come about because of Nineveh's many harlotries and sorceries used to sell nations.

Yahweh intervenes with an oracle. He is against Nineveh and will humiliate her before the nations. All who see the devastation will flee in horror. From where can Yahweh find someone to lament and comfort her? There is no one.

Nahum returns to complete the prophecy. Is Nineveh and her gods any better than Thebes, capital of Egypt, and its god Amon Rē, that sat by canals of the Nile? Ethiopia and all Egypt were her might, with Put and the Libyans her helpers. Assurbanipal destroyed that great city and carried captives into exile. Her little ones were dashed in pieces, and over her honored ones, bound in chains, lots were cast.

Nineveh too will drink, stagger, and become unconscious, seeking some dwelling place among the enemy but probably not finding one. Her celebrated fortresses are compared by the prophet to fig trees with first-ripe figs. If the fig tree is shaken figs will fall easily into the mouth of the eater. Nineveh's outer gates are now wide open and their bars burned. Nahum calls attention to Nineveh's troops who have become like weak women. With the outer defenses now open to the enemy, Ninevites are told to draw water for the siege, strengthen the forts, and make bricks to repair breeches in the city wall. But it will be to no avail. Fire and sword will consume the defenders like young locusts. Multiply yourself for the slaughter! the prophet says. Nineveh's traders, princes, and scribes will vanish like locusts on a cold stone wall when the sun rises. They will go to who knows where.

The prophecy has a closing word for the king of Assyria. His officials and nobles lie dead on the mountains with none to gather them. There is no one to alleviate the king's wound. Everyone who hears news of Nineveh's fall will hiss and clap their hands in derision, for upon whom has not passed the king's cruelty?

This collection of Nahum's prophecies has no overall structure like the core prophecies of Habakkuk 1–2. Instead all are connected by catchwords.

When comparing Nahum's prophecies to those of Jeremiah, it is interesting to note that while both prophets were active when Nineveh fell, Nahum makes this his one-theme prophecy, while Jeremiah in many more prophecies says nothing about it! Zephaniah, an earlier contemporary of both, does anticipate the fall of Assyria (Zeph 2:13–15).

## HABAKKUK

The superscription to the book of Habakkuk provides no information about this prophet. Superscriptions to most Minor and Major Prophets, with the exception of Habakkuk, Obadiah, and Joel, provide readers with one or more of the following: the prophet's family connections; where the prophet came from; when or how the call to the prophetic office came about (Amos, Jeremiah, Ezekiel); under what king or kings the prophet prophesied; what other notable events happened during the prophet's ministry (Amos); or to what audience the prophet's words were directed.

Habakkuk can confidently be dated to the reign of Jehoiakim (605–598), i.e., the very end of the seventh century. Haak[9] dates Habakkuk ca. 605–603. After 609 the Assyrians have vanished from the world scene, so go unmentioned by the prophet. Focus of attention is on the Chaldeans/Babylonians, now the main power-broker in the ANE and a real threat to Judah and Jerusalem.

After a brief complaint by Habakkuk about the violence and mischief rife in Jerusalem, and Yahweh seemingly

9. Haak, *Habakkuk*, 154.

not hearing the prophet's cries, Yahweh answers by saying he is rousing the ruthless Chaldeans, who seize dwellings and are answerable only to themselves (1:5–11). The ensuing dialogue remains focused on the Babylonian threat (1:12—2:5), ending climactically with Habakkuk hurling five woes upon the Babylonians and their king (2:6–20).

Jeremiah, too, anticipated a Babylonian threat but it came earlier—at the time of his commissioning sometime after 622 (Jer 1:13–19).[10] He had much to say about this threat in his early "foe" oracles (4:5–21, 23–31; 5:1–19; 6:1–12, 22–26), but for him the Babylonians would be more than a threat: they would bring judgment upon Judah, and the nation's only hope was to repent from wrongdoing. Habakkuk says nothing specific about the Babylonians coming to judge Judah and makes no calls for repentance.

Habakkuk, however, was not circumspect about Babylon and its king being readied for divine judgment. His woe oracles in chapter 2 contain the specificity common to Jeremiah's oracles against Judah. But with Habakkuk we do not know if judgment on Babylon will take place in the near or distant future. The prophet is simply told to wait for a promised vision to be fulfilled, and that "the righteous will live by his faithfulness" (Hab 2:2–4). He sounds more like Isaiah here than Jeremiah. Isaiah counseled King Hezekiah to wait out the Assyrian threat, for the enemy would return home, which is precisely what happened (2 Kgs 19:1–36). Did Habakkuk think, too, that Yahweh would soon deliver Judah from Nebuchadnezzar and the Babylonians, and that judgment on Babylon would follow as a matter of course? Long before 598, when Nebuchadnezzar first visited Jerusalem, Jeremiah knew judgment, not deliverance, was in store for Judah. Deliverance would be a long ways

10. Lundbom, "Rhetorical Structures in Jeremiah"; Lundbom, *Jeremiah 1–20*, 248.

off (Jer 29:10–14). Jeremiah, who also delivered oracles of judgment against Babylon (Jer 50:1—51:58; cf. 25:26b), predicted a stereotypical 70-year tenure for Babylon as a world power (Jer 25:11–14), which turned out to be a good approximation.[11] Judgment would come upon Babylon once Yahweh had brought judgment upon Judah.

Differences between the prophecies of Jeremiah and Habakkuk doubtless had much to do with their both having been spoken during the reign of Jehoiakim. Jehoiakim was put on the throne by an Egyptian Pharaoh, and for the first part of his reign was beholden to him, perhaps also during the short time he pledged obedience to the Babylonian king. Insecure as he was, Jehoiakim would probably not have been threatened by an indeterminate prophecy against Babylon. Jeremiah's scroll of judgment oracles against Judah, read publicly by Baruch in the temple in 605, so threatened Jehoiakim that he and Baruch had to go into hiding. It is good they did, for when Jehoiakim heard words of the scroll he had the scroll cut into strips and cast into the fire. The king then sought to arrest Baruch and Jeremiah, but "Yahweh hid them" (Jer 36:1–26). Jeremiah also spoke "woe" and "non-woe" oracles against this unjust, violent, and oppressive monarch (Jer 22:13–19), which would have infuriated Jehoiakim had they been reported to him. Jeremiah's oracle portending a rapid defeat of Egypt by the Babylonians would further have infuriated Jehoiakim (Jer 46:2–24). On Jehoiakim's treatment of Uriah of Kiraith-jearim, who spoke words similar to those of Jeremiah, see below.

Habakkuk's words about "waiting" reflect a theme prominent in Isaiah:

---

11. Lundbom, *Jeremiah 1–20*, 249–50.

| Isa 8:17 | I will wait for Yahweh | Hab 2:3 | If it seems to tarry, wait for it |
| Isa 30:18 | Therefore Yahweh wait to be gracious to you ... blessed are all those who wait for him | Hab 3:16 | I wait quietly for the day of calamity |

Habakkuk's core prophecy in chapters 1–2 is a dialogue. Chapter 3 is an added psalm said to have been spoken or sung by the prophet. The core prophecy has the following structure, which may or may not point to the oracles having been spoken in sequence:

A    Habakkuk: Why am I made to see all this *violence* and wrongdoing? (1:2–4)
   B    Yahweh: I am rousing the fierce and impetuous Chaldeans (1:5–11)
      C    Habakkuk: But are they to keep on destroying nations? (1:12–17)
      C'    Habakkuk: I will stand at the watchtower and await an answer (2:1)
   B'    Yahweh: The righteous will live by his faithfulness (2:2–5)
A'    Habakkuk: Woe to those engaged in *violence* and wrongdoing (2:6b–20)

Habakkuk begins and ends as speaker; in the center it is Yahweh, Habakkuk, Habakkuk, and Yahweh speaking (chiasmus). The prophet begins by asking Yahweh why the prophet himself must look upon all the violence and wrongdoing in Jerusalem. Yahweh answers, saying he is already taking care of this by raising up an enemy, and it is a fierce enemy that gathers captives like sand. Okay, but if this enemy swallows up nation after nation, Habakkuk wants to know, will the carnage go on indefinitely? What is not said, but what one can well imagine in the prophet's mind, is the question: What will happen to Judah, the lone survivor of Yahweh's covenant people?

Habakkuk ascends a watchtower, hoping to receive an answer to this question, after which he will give a response. Yahweh is quick to answer. He tells the prophet to write the received revelation plainly and in large letters—large enough so one running by can read it. It may take time, but fulfilled it will be! The prophet is to wait even if the revelation seems to tarry. The revelation is this: "Look, the puffed up one—his soul is not right in him, but the righteous will live by his faithfulness." As for haughty soldiers of the Babylonian army, they will become drunk as on wine, and though their appetite to conquer is never satisfied, they will not endure.

What is the prophet's response? It is a litany of woes upon those engaged in greed, violence, human bloodshed, and other wrongdoings, who are the Babylonians. The last woe pokes fun at idols, their makers, and priests who give oracles by them. The prophet closes with this confession: "But Yahweh is in his holy temple. Keep silent before him all the earth!"

This concluding confession, which has become a signature of the prophet, has a twofold function. The first is that it contrasts Yahweh, alive is he in his holy temple (cf. Ps 11:4a), to inert idols worshiped in Babylon and by the king of Babylon. The second is that in it Habakkuk answers his opening outcry in 1:2–4. He began by complaining that he had been crying to Yahweh about violence and wrongdoing in Jerusalem, and Yahweh was not listening. Yahweh remained silent! Where was Yahweh anyway? Now he answers himself: Yahweh is in his holy temple, everyone including himself is to be *silent* before him!

An added psalm in chapter 3 celebrates Yahweh's mighty acts from hoary antiquity—against nations and for Israel's salvation.

## OTHER PROPHETS OF THE SEVENTH CENTURY

### Jeremiah

The dominant prophet of the seventh century and beyond was Jeremiah, preaching a reform message and imminent judgment to Jerusalem and Judah during Josiah's reign (622–609). He was active but persecuted during Jehoiakim's early years (609–605). Then he was out of public view for seven years after dictating his first scroll to Baruch (604–597). But he became active again early in the reign of weak Zedekiah (597–594/3). Then for another seven years (594–588) no definite knowledge of the prophet's activity has come to light. In the end he was imprisoned or confined to the court of the guard until Jerusalem fell to the Babylonians in 587/6. Jeremiah survived the fall and was released by Nebuzaradan under instructions of the Babylonian king (39:11–14; 40:1–6), after which he joined the remnant community at Mizpah, led by the Babylonian-appointed governor, Gedaliah—son of Ahikam, son of Shaphan—where he and Baruch remained roughly four years.[12] The community was fractured by the murder of Gedaliah (41:1–3), after which Baruch and Jeremiah were taken with others to Egypt where they settled at Tahpanhes in the Nile Delta (43:7). In Egypt Jeremiah preached to Judahites who sought refuge there during the last, chaotic years of Judah, and the prophet spent his final days there.

That Jeremiah was remembered as a figure larger than life is due, no doubt, to the fact that he was indeed

12. Lundbom, *Jeremiah 1–20*, 120.

a remarkable individual who lived an authentic life and preached an authentic word from Yahweh during Israel's final years of nationhood. But the prophet's legacy is also due in no small part to the work of Baruch ben Neriah, a professional Jerusalem scribe who became an associate of Jeremiah at some point in his mid-career, and is doubtless the one responsible for writing and editing the book bearing the prophet's name (36). For no other Hebrew prophet do we possess a comparable amount of collected preaching; historical and biographical information; dated accounts; symbolic acts (13:1–11, 12–14; 16:1–4, 5–7, 8–9; 19:1–13; 25:15–29; 27–28; 32; 35:1–11; 43:8–13); and interactions with kings (21:3–7; 22:1–5; 27:12–15; 34:1–7; 37:17–20; 38:14–28), royal officials and leading citizens (25:12–15; 26:12–15; 37:3–8, 12–16; 38:1–6; 42:1–22; 43:1–4), palace domestics (38:7–13; 39:15–18), foreign envoys (27:1–11). We also have accounts of Jeremiah's encounters with a Babylonian official (39:11–14; 40:1–6), with priestly kin at Anathoth (11:18–12:6; 32:6–12), with priests in Jerusalem (19:1—20:6; 21:1–2; 26:7–11; 27:16–22; 29:29–32; 37:3–11), with prophets in Jerusalem (26:7–11; 28), and with the Rechabites (35) and Judahite exiles in Egypt (43:8–13; 44:1–25). Also, preaching against kings (21:1—23:8) and prophets (23:9–40) were compiled into separate collections. Baruch's brother, Seraiah, also a trained scribe in the employ of King Zedekiah, assisted in preserving a smaller part of the Jeremiah legacy (51:59–64).

From the superscription to the Jeremiah book we learn that the prophet was a son of Hilkiah belonging to a priestly family living in the town of Anathoth, approximately three miles north of Jerusalem. Anathoth was in the old territory of Benjamin, the southernmost part of Northern Israel where northern traditions were preserved, the most important of which were those connected with Israel's first sanctuary at Shiloh. Shiloh is where Samuel grew up a boy under Eli the priest (1 Sam 3). The line through Samuel picked up even more prestige when traced further back to Moses.

Jeremiah was called to be Yahweh's prophet before he was born, the call coming to him in the thirteenth year of Josiah's reign, which was 628/27. The boy resisted, but Yahweh overruled him, saying that on this day he was putting his words into Jeremiah's mouth and appointing him over nations and kingdoms "to uproot and break down, to destroy and overthrow, to build up and plant" (1:9–10). Jeremiah was to be the "prophet like Moses" (Deut 18:18). It was, however, a promissory word, with Yahweh adding, "I am watching over my word to do it" (1:12). So far as Jeremiah was concerned, he refrained from giving an acceptance. That, too, would come only later.

Acceptance of the call came with the finding of the lawbook in the temple in 622 (2 Kgs 22:3–20). Jeremiah in a later reflection said: "Your words were found and I ate them, and your word was to me for joy, and for the gladness of my heart" (15:16). These were the words Yahweh promised to put into Jeremiah's mouth (1:9). Sometime later Jeremiah was commissioned to be Yahweh's prophet (1:13–19), and he began (1) preaching in support of Josiah's reform, according to which pagan religious practices were denounced and repentance was called for; and (2) warning inhabitants of Jerusalem and Judah that a foe was on the horizon waiting to bring judgment on those forsaking Yahweh, making offerings to other gods, and worshiping the work of their hands (1:13–16). The coming of a foe also necessitated making laments. Jeremiah's preaching during the reign of Josiah, except for the two-sister allegory in 3:6–11, is undated. But more than likely it consisted of two early collections: an "apostasy-repentance cycle" (2:1—4:4) and a "foe-lament cycle" (4:5—9:22 [Heb 9:21]; 10:17–22).[13]

The remainder of chapters 11–20 contains a substratum of confessions along with various other preaching. In the later years of Josiah and early years of Jehoiakim the prophet poured out his soul to Yahweh in words much like those appearing in the Psalms. Jeremiah was a man of prayer. Chapters 1–20 are the first identifiable book of Jeremiah, tied together as they are by an inclusio. Jeremiah's final words of lament in 20:18 are answered by the opening words of his call:[14]

> Why this: *from the womb / came I forth*
>    to see hard times and sorrow
>       and my days end in shame?
>          (20:18)

> Before I formed you in the belly I knew you
>    and before *you came forth / from the womb* I
> declared you holy
>    a prophet to the nations I made you
>       (1:5)

During Josiah's reign Jeremiah appears to have hoped for a return of exiles from Assyria (3:12–18; 30:18–21; 31:2–14, 16–20), and these are combined with hope oracles for Judah in the "Book of Restoration" (30–33).

Jeremiah is silent about Josiah's misadventure to Megiddo. The Deuteronomic History also offers no explanation. The Chronicler belated says that Josiah "did not listen to the words of Neco from the mouth of God" (2 Chr 35:22). Jeremiah did, however, utter a lament for Josiah (2 Chr 35:25).

---

13. Lundbom, *Jeremiah 1–20*, 94.
14. Lundbom, *Jeremiah 1–20*, 93–95.

The years from 609–605 under King Jehoiakim were difficult for the prophet. The reform had come to a full stop, and in Jehoiakim's accession year the prophet delivered his riveting Temple Oracles (7:3–14; 26:1–19), which were a scathing indictment on people's shallow religiosity and duplicity before Yahweh. A nerve was struck when Jeremiah said Yahweh would destroy the temple as he had Israel's first sanctuary at Shiloh. Court was called into session at the New Gate and Jeremiah was put on trial for his life. Priests and prophets made up the prosecution, calling for Jeremiah's death. But the princes who were to decide the case acquitted the prophet on the strength of his testimony that Yahweh had sent him with the message he delivered. Elders in attendance also spoke up in Jeremiah's defense, and his friend Ahiakim son of Shaphan provided him protection in the days following (26:24).

Jeremiah dictated his first scroll—which may have been substantially less than 1–20—to Baruch in 605 when Nebuchadnezzar had just delivered Neco and the Egyptians a crushing defeat at Carchemish, and in a couple years would be in the Philistine Plain laying waste to Ashkelon and Ekron, events easily believed to be a real threat to the security of Jerusalem (36:1–8). Baruch took the scroll by dictation and was instructed by Jeremiah to read it in the temple on an anticipated fast day when a large number of people would be present. He read it the following year. Colleagues knew the scroll would have to be read to King Jehoiakim. It was, and upon hearing Jeremiah's words the king consigned them strip by strip to the brazier before which he was sitting in his winter house (36:9–26). The scroll was later rewritten by Baruch and expanded with more words (36:27–32). Jeremiah and Baruch were advised to go into hiding, which they did (36:19), and the prophet did not emerge in public until after Jehoiakim met his end, the Babylonians were at the doorstep of Jerusalem, and Jeremiah had advised young Jehoiachin and the queen mother to step down, take a seat on the ground, and surrender (13:18–20), which they did. The city surrendered to Nebuchadnezzar in 597. The prophet's message to departing exiles was hopeful, but bittersweet (31:21–22).

Nebuchadnezzar took King Jehoiachin and the queen mother, leading citizens, artisans, and smiths to Babylon. Jeremiah later wrote the exiles a couple letters advising them to settle down, pray for the welfare of the city, and wait for Yahweh's deliverance—and saying that in seventy years Yahweh would bring their descendants back to the land (29).

Persecution of the prophet began early, coming during Josiah's reign but intensifying during the early years of Jehoiakim when Jerusalem was tottering on the verge of collapse. Early on Jeremiah incurred the wrath of kin at Anathoth, perhaps because he supported Josiah's program of centralized worship in Jerusalem, which would have effectively shut down the Anathoth sanctuary. The prophet says he was "like a lamb led to the slaughter" (11:18–27; cf. 12:5–6). At some point in his early career plots were made against Jeremiah by priests, prophets, and the wise, and a pit was dug for his life (18:19–23).

Jeremiah endured even more persecution during the reign of Jehoiakim (15:10, 15, 20–21). Early in the king's reign, probably ca. 605, Jeremiah took some priests and elders out to Potsherd Gate where he broke a pottery jug to dramatize Yahweh's outrage at the pagan worship being carried on in the Valley of Ben-Hinnom, which included child sacrifice (19:1–13). Jeremiah later preached the same message in the temple courtyard, and the priest Pashhur, who was chief overseer of the temple, struck the prophet and put him in the stocks in the Upper Benjamin Gate, where he remained overnight (cf. 2 Chr 16:10). When released in the morning, Jeremiah returned the favor by giving Pashhur a stinging rebuke of himself and his family (19:14—20:6).

In a confession about the same time, Jeremiah complained directly to Yahweh about his call to prophesy and said that speaking Yahweh's word had brought him nothing but derision. He could hear whisperings in the crowd, "Terror on every side," one of his sayings now being applied to him as a taunt. All his trusted friends were watching for his fall (20:7–10). But he follows this with another confession expressing confidence and celebrating deliverance from the crisis, for the plot apparently did not succeed (20:11–13). These confessions could date from 609 when Jeremiah was put on trial for his life and the verdict was an acquittal, or else in 604 when his first scroll was read publicly and protection was given the prophet after the scroll was read to the king. In another heart-wrenching confession, dated possibly ca. 605–4 when hostilities peaked between Jehoiakim and the prophet, Jeremiah cursed the day he was born (20:14–18).

Jeremiah endured another round of hard times under Zedekiah when he had become the key figure in the tragic drama that was unfolding. During the first four years of this king, when the prophet was active (597–594/3) the prophecy about good and bad figs was given—the good figs being those taken to Babylon in the exile of 597, and the bad figs being those remaining in Jerusalem (24). At the beginning of Zedekiah's reign Jeremiah wore a yoke bar and prophesied submission to Nebuchadnezzar, first to foreign envoys present in Jerusalem planning a rebellion, then to Zedekiah, and then to priests and all the people (27). This was followed by a confrontation in the temple between Jeremiah and the prophet Hananiah of Gibeon, where the latter broke the yoke bar from off Jeremiah's neck. Jeremiah later returned to rain judgment on Hananiah, saying he was preaching a lie and would die. In two months the prophet Hananiah was dead (28).

During Zedekiah's final years (588–587/6) the prophet continued speaking to the king and people of Jerusalem, being in and out of prison, and twice confined to the court of the guard. In the court of the guard he could receive visitors and speak both about imminent judgment and hope for the future. The so-called "via dolorosa" prose of 37:1—38:28 records Jeremiah's final days of suffering and documents his entire life as a symbolic act in the service of Yahweh.

When the city was under siege Zedekiah brokered a covenant whereby slaveowners—including himself—would grant liberty to all their Hebrew slaves, But when Egypt marched north and forced the Babylonians to retreat, slaveowners reneged on the covenant and took back their slaves. Jeremiah was swift with a word of judgment to Zedekiah and his fellow schemers (34:8–22).

During a lifting of the siege Jeremiah attempted to go to Anathoth to take care of some personal business, but when he got to the Benjamin Gate he was arrested by a sentinel and charged with desertion. Jeremiah denied the charges but was turned over to princes, who beat him and cast him into a cistern in the house of Jonathan the scribe, which had been made into a prison. There he remained for many days until Zedekiah secretly sought him out for a word from Yahweh, and although it was not a word the king wanted to hear, he nevertheless granted the prophet's request not to be returned to prison (37:11–21). Jeremiah was then placed under house arrest in the court of the guard.

It happened also when certain individuals heard Jeremiah preaching surrender to the Babylonians that they told the king this was weakening the morale of soldiers defending the city, and could not be tolerated. The king said he could do nothing, and gave Jeremiah over to the men. They cast him into an empty cistern of Malchiah, where he sank in the mud. But rescue this time came in dramatic fashion. Ebed-melech the Cushite, who was a domestic employed in the palace, heard what had happened and went straightaway to the king, who was deciding cases in the Benjamin Gate. He told the king that wicked men had cast Jeremiah into a pit and he would die there of hunger. So the king told Ebed-melech to round up thirty men and pull Jeremiah out. This was done, and Jeremiah once again was returned to the court of the guard (38:1–13). Jeremiah later promised deliverance to Ebed-melech (39:15–18) as he did also to his friend Baruch, who lamented not having achieved greatness in life and in its place had come only sorrow added to pain (45).

The prophet gave some important prophecies during this difficult time. On the other side of doom would be deliverance and restoration. Jeremiah's most important prophecy was one about a "new covenant" that would be fulfilled in future days, replacing the covenant people had broken (31:31–34). Elsewhere it is called an "eternal covenant" (32:40; 50:5). This covenant was later believed to have been fulfilled in the life, death, and resurrection of Jesus the Christ. Other hopeful prophecies may derive from this same period (23:5–8; 31:23–40; 33:1–26) or from an earlier time when Judahites were facing exile (16:14–15, 19–21).

Jeremiah while confined to the court of the guard bought a field at Anathoth from his cousin Hanamel at a time when buying property, especially when Babylonian soldiers were probably encamped on it, was sheer foolishness. Nevertheless the transaction was completed with the assistance of Baruch and in the presence of Judahites who acted as witnesses, and Jeremiah said it would be a sign that houses, fields, and vineyards would again be bought in the land (32:6–15).

Jeremiah survived the destruction of Jerusalem in 587 and was released at the command of Nebuchadnezzar, left to join the remnant community at Mizpah (39:11–14; 40:1–6). His own life he was given as a "trophy of war" (39:18; 45:5), and earlier promises to him from Yahweh were now seen as having been fulfilled (1:18, 19; 15:20–21). Jeremiah and Baruch remained roughly four years at Mizpah, until Gedaliah (40:7–12), the Babylonian-appointed governor, was murdered along with others in a plot instigated by the king of Ammon (40:13—41:3). A company under the direction of Johanan son of Kareah then fled to Geruth Chimham near Bethlehem, and later journeyed on to Egypt, taking Jeremiah and Baruch with them (41:16—43:7).

In Egypt Jeremiah preached judgment to Jewish exiles engaged in the same Queen of Heaven (= Ashtart) worship carried on earlier in Jerusalem. He also performed a symbolic act to show that King Nebuchadnezzar would come to Egypt and kindle a fire in the temples of the gods of Egypt and break the obelisks of Heliopolis (43–44). The prophet is last heard from in Egypt (43:8—44:30), and the Bible does not record his death.

Jeremiah was appointed by Yahweh in his call to be a prophet to the nations (1:4), to preach judgment and hope to nations and kingdoms of the world (1:10). Like other prophets he spoke mainly judgment upon foreign nations—in 9:25–26 [Heb 9:24–25]; 10:25; in his "cup of wrath" vision (25:15–29); and in a substantial collection of Foreign Nation oracles (46–51 MT). Distant hope was preached to only a few of these nations (46:26b; 48:47; 49:6, 11; 49:39).

Jeremiah's understanding of himself as "the prophet like Moses" led him to be mediator of the covenant, a role in which he sought to plead the people's case to Yahweh when estrangement occurred or when judgment was imminent.[15] In Jeremiah's last years he was asked often to mediate for King Zedekiah and the people when Judah was threatened by the Babylonians. However, as we shall see, Jeremiah did not enjoy Moses's success as a covenant mediator.

The covenant mediator *par excellence* in the Old Testament was Moses, called upon to negotiate disputes between Israel and the Egyptian Pharaoh, and even more between Yahweh and Israel during the period of wilderness wanderings. Moses had a mediating role before the Exodus when Yahweh sent him to the Pharaoh and the Israelites to announce his plan to deliver Israel out of slavery (Exod 3:7–22), apparently not wanting to speak to either party directly. Mediation took time and required a series of terrible plagues to wear the Pharaoh down, but in the end it was successful.

At Sinai Moses became a mediator when a theophany occurred leaving the people rocking in fright. The Ten Commandments were given as the people stood at a safe distance. Moses, not Yahweh, was asked to speak to them lest they die (Exod 19:16–19; 20:18–19; Deut 4:9–14, 32–40; 5:2–5, 22–27). Mediation was again necessary after Moses ascended the mountain and in his absence the people fashioned a golden calf. Yahweh this time was so wroth with the people that he wanted to destroy them, but Moses pleaded their case, made atonement for their sin, and the mediation was successful. Yahweh forgave the people, the covenant was renewed, and Israel was allowed to resume its journey (Exod 32:11–14, 30–32; 33:1–17; Deut 9:7–21; 10:10–11).

Moses had to intercede for Israel a number of other times in the wilderness: when the people complained about their misfortune at Taberah (Num 11:1–3; Deut 9:22–29); when the people rejected the returning spies who had gone

15. Lundbom, "Jeremiah as Covenant Mediator," 437–54.

to scope out Canaan, and wanted to replace Moses and Aaron with another leader. But again Moses mediated the dispute and the people were pardoned (Num 13-14; Deut 1:26-46). There was also the rebellion of Korah. This time both Moses and Aaron had to intercede, with the result that Korah and his followers were swallowed up into the earth. But the rebellion was not over. People continued to murmur against Moses and Aaron and Yahweh sent a plague. But Moses and Aaron made atonement for the people, their mediation was successful, and the plague was halted (Numbers 16). Samuel, too, we should note, was remembered as another important mediator between Yahweh and the people (1 Sam 7:7-11; 8:4-9; 12:7-25; Jer 15:1).

In Jeremiah's early years mediation appears to have been sought in public worship. In 3:21-25 his call for a faithless people to return (= repent) is answered by a confession of sin on the part of the people. If Jeremiah happens to have been the liturgist, he would have been acting as mediator of the covenant. The corporate confession is later expanded in 3:24-25. Other communal laments in 14:7-9 and 20-22 may also have been recited in public worship.

Elsewhere in the early poetry are laments, confessions, and rejections of mediation. Jeremiah in a personal confession says he stood before Yahweh to speak good for individuals who had dug a pit to take his life, asking Yahweh to take away his wrath from them (18:19-23). Whether his mediation was successful the text does not say. Probably it was not, for the plots continued (18:18).

In 14:1-6 is a lament over a drought that was particularly severe. What follows is another communal confession and a petition for deliverance, which also could have been led by Jeremiah (14:7-9). But this time Yahweh answered with two judgment oracles—one for the nation and one for prophets preaching peace (14:10, 15-16). Mediation was rejected; Yahweh would not listen to Jeremiah as he did to Moses. On another occasion it happened all over again. Jeremiah uttered a personal lament (14:17–19b) followed by a communal lament and confession of sin (14:19–22), after which came a judgment oracle and Jeremiah's most emphatic rejection as covenant mediator. The prophet says:

> And Yahweh said to me: If Moses and Samuel were to stand before me, my soul would not incline to this people. Send them from my presence. And let them go out. And it will happen when they say to you, "Where shall we go out?" then you shall say to them:
> Thus said Yahweh:
> Whoever is to death—to death, and whoever is to the sword—to the sword, and whoever is to famine—to famine, and whoever is to captivity—to captivity. And I will appoint over them four families—oracle of Yahweh—the sword to kill and the dogs to drag away; and the birds of the skies and the beasts of the earth to devour and to destroy. (15:1–3)

Other rejections of mediation occurred early in the reign of Jehoiakim. After Jeremiah gave his Temple Oracles in 609, Yahweh told him not to pray for the people, not to raise a cry on their behalf, not to intercede with him because he would not listen (7:16). Similar directives occurred in 11:14 and 14:11. Jeremiah did not enjoy Moses' success as covenant mediator.

In the reign of Zedekiah, the king asked Jeremiah to mediate on his and the nation's behalf, hoping against hope that the Babylonians currently besieging Jerusalem would turn around and go home (21:1–7; 37:3–10). Jeremiah's mediation in each case was answered with a divine "No!" Before the fall of Jerusalem the "prophet like Moses" announced a new covenant from his place of confinement in the court of the guard and in so doing was acting like Moses as covenant mediator (31:31–34). Then after the fall of Jerusalem, when the remnant community had fled Mizpah following the murder of Gedaliah, and had a mind to go to Egypt (41:17), it was decided they should first ask Jeremiah to pray to Yahweh on their behalf. They did this, and Jeremiah put the matter before Yahweh. He had to wait ten days for an answer. Yahweh said the people should not go to Egypt, but should remain in the land. But Jeremiah's mediation was again rejected, this time by the people who refused to listen and instead accused the prophet of telling them a lie. The group headed for Egypt (42:1—43:7).

## Huldah

After the lawbook was found in the temple in 622, the prophetess Huldah was consulted. After reading it or hearing it read she preached riveting judgment on Judah, but had a redemptive word for Josiah. He had humbled himself, and Huldah said he would die in peace, not seeing the disaster about to come upon Jerusalem (2 Kgs 22:14–20).

## Uriah

Uriah, a prophet from Kiraith-jearim, spoke words similar to those of Jeremiah and had to flee to Egypt because Jehoiakim threatened him with death. Egypt, however, was the wrong place to go. With Jehoiakim beholden to the Pharaoh, Uriah's extradition back to Judah was a simple matter. He was returned to Jerusalem where Jehoiakim put him to death after which the king unceremoniously cast Uriah's dead body into the burial ground for commoners (Jer 26:20–23).

## TIMELINE OF THE LATE SEVENTH CENTURY

- 642 King Manasseh of Judah dies (2 Kgs 21:18; 2 Chr 33:20) Amon is made king in Judah but is assassinated after two years by an anti-Assyrian party; those responsible are quickly punished (2 Kgs 21:19–24; 2 Chr 33:21–25).
- 640 Josiah is made king in Judah at eight years old (2 Kgs 21:24; 2 Chr 34:1).
- 632 Josiah while still a boy begins to seek Yahweh (2 Chr 34:3a).
- 628 Josiah begins a purge of false worship in Judah (2 Kgs 23:4–20, 24; 2 Chr 34:3b–7).

    Zephaniah begins preaching in support of Josiah's reform.
- 627 King Assurbanipal of Assyria dies (Haran Inscription). Jeremiah is called to be a prophet as a boy in 13th year of Josiah (Jer 1:2, 4–12); he may have begun to hear the preaching of Zephaniah.
- 626 Nabopolassar defeats an Assyrian army outside of Babylon; a month later he declares himself King of Babylon.
- 622 A lawbook is found in the Jerusalem temple (2 Kgs 22:3–13; 2 Chr 34:8–21)

    Huldah gives prophecy for Judah and King Josiah (2 Kgs 22:14–20; 2 Chr 34:22–28)

    A covenant renewal ceremony takes place in Jerusalem (2 Kgs 23:1–3; 2 Chr 34:29–33)

    A grand Passover is celebrated in Jerusalem (2 Kgs 23:21–23; 2 Chr 35:1–19).

    Jeremiah accepts call to be a prophet (Jer 15:16)
    Jeremiah is commissioned as a prophet of Yahweh (Jer 1:13–19); he begins preaching shortly thereafter.
- 612 Nineveh falls to a coalition of Babylonians and Medes.

Nahum prophesies the fall of Nineveh, perhaps just before 612.

609 An Assyrian remnant is defeated at Haran; Josiah is killed by Pharaoh Neco of Egypt at Megiddo, is taken to Jerusalem, dies, and is buried (2 Kgs 23:29–30; 2 Chr 35:20–24). Jeremiah utters a lament over Josiah (2 Chr 35:25).

Jehoahaz is put on the Jerusalem throne; he is deposed by Neco after three months and taken away to Egypt (2 Kgs 23:31–33; 34b; 2 Chr 36:1–3, 4b). Neco places Jehoiakim is on the throne (2 Kgs 23:34a; 2 Chr 36:4a).

Jeremiah preaches Temple Oracles in Jehoiakim's accession year, is put on trial for his life, but is acquitted (Jer 7:3–14; 26:1–19, 24).

Uriah of Kiriath-jearim preaches judgment against Jerusalem, flees to Egypt to escape wrath of Jehoiakim, but is brought back and put to death (Jer 26:20–23).

605 Nebuchadnezzar II defeats Egyptians at Carchemish (Jer 46:2).

Habakkuk begins preaching in Jerusalem.

604 Nebuchadnezzar, now in the Philistine Plain, destroys Ashkelon (Jer 47)

Jehoiakim proclaims a fast in Jerusalem (Jer 36:9) and transfers his allegiance to Babylon (2 Kgs 24:1).

Jeremiah has a collection of oracles read by Baruch in the temple on a fast day (Jer 36:1–10); Jehoiakim's rage is anticipated; Jeremiah and Baruch are advised to go into hiding (Jer 36:11–19); Jehoiakim hears the scroll read and consigns it to the flames (Jer 36:20–26).

603 Nebuchadnezzar destroys Philistine Ekron.

601 Jehoiakim declares independence from Babylon (2 Kgs 24:1).

598 In December, Nebuchadnezzar and the full Babylonian army arrive in Jerusalem (2 Kgs 24:10–11); Jehoiakim dies; likely assassinated (2 Kgs 24:6; cf. Jer 22:18–19; 36:30); the Chronicler says he was bound to be taken to Babylon (2 Chr 36:6).

Young Jehoiachin is put on the Jerusalem throne but is deposed by Nebuchadnezzar after three months and taken away to Babylon (2 Kgs 24:8; 2 Chr 36:9–10a)

> Jeremiah comes out of hiding and advises the king and the queen mother to surrender (Jer 13:18–20).

597 In March Jerusalem surrenders to Nebuchadnezzar; the temple and palace are looted of treasures, and King Jehoiachin, the queen mother, and prominent citizens are taken into exile (2 Kgs 24:12–16; Jer 29:2; 2 Chr 36:7); Nebuchadnezzar puts Zedekiah on the Jerusalem throne (2 Kgs 24:17; 2 Chr 36:10)

## REFLECTION

1. Would you agree with Abraham Heschel that the prophets show a love of kindness?

2. Would you agree with Abraham Heschel that with divine anger also comes divine mercy? Are judges today expected to temper judgments with mercy?

3. Zephaniah called on people to wait for the Lord, an earlier and important theme of the prophet Isaiah. How long do you think they had to wait for the Lord to change the speech of all peoples to a pure speech, and for Jerusalem to shout and be glad because the Lord had commuted her sentence?

4. Jeremiah was fearless in confronting Jehoiakim and his beloved nation with a multitude of the monarch's own wrongdoings. Might there have been an understandable caution on the part of Nahum and Habakkuk, who prophesied at the same time, to address the same topics?

# ZEPHANIAH

# 3

# "THE DAY OF YAHWEH IS AT HAND" (1:2-18)

1 *²I will utterly sweep away everything*
*from upon the face of the earth, oracle of Yahweh*
*³I will sweep away humans and beasts*
*I will sweep away birds of the heavens and fish of the sea*
*and the stumbling blocks with the wicked*[1]
*And I will cut off humans*
*from upon the face of the earth, oracle of Yahweh*
*⁴I will stretch out my hand upon Judah*
*and upon all the inhabitants of Jerusalem*
*And I will cut off from this place*
*the remnant of Baal*
*the name of the Chemarim*[2] *with the priests*

1. The line is difficult, although Driver reads the MT; "stumbling blocks" could be idols (cf. Ezek 14:4-7), and the wicked with them. The line is otherwise read "I will overthrow the wicked" (RSV) or "I will make the wicked stumble" (NRSV).

2. An Aramaic word denoting idolatrous priests of foreign cults (Driver).

> [5] *And those who bow down upon the roofs to the host of heaven*[3]
>> *and those who bow down, who swear to Yahweh*
>> *and who swear by Milcom*[4]
> [6] *Yes, those who have turned away from following Yahweh*
>> *and who do not seek Yahweh and do not inquire*
>
> [7] *Keep silent at the presence of Lord Yahweh!*
>> *for the day of Yahweh is at hand*
> *For Yahweh has prepared a sacrifice*
>> *he has consecrated his invited ones*
>
> [8] *And it will be on the day of Yahweh's sacrifice*
>> *that I will visit the officials*[5] *and the king's sons*
>>> *and all those clothed in foreign attire*
> [9] *And I will visit all who leap over the threshold*[6]
>> *on that day*
>>> *those who fill their master's house with violence and deceit*
> [10] *And it will be on that day, oracle of Yahweh*
>> *the sound of a cry from the Fish Gate*

---

3. I.e., the heavenly bodies (Deut 4:19; 17:3; 2 Kgs 21:3, 5; Jer 8:1–2). This may also be the Assyrian Queen of Heaven cult mentioned in Jer 7:18 and 44:15–25 (Lundbom, *Jeremiah 1–20*, 476).

4. Reading with the LXX and the Versions. MT with a different pointing has "their king." Milcom was god of the Ammonites, and Solomon in his later years brought worship of this deity to Jerusalem (1 Kgs 11:5, 33). Josiah in his reform tore down worship sites for Milcom (2 Kgs 23:13).

5. Or "princes." Royal families were large due to kings having many wives. It is also argued that the term "king's son" may refer simply to a low-ranking court official, one who is not an actual son of a king (Driver). The subject is debated (cf. Lundbom, *Jeremiah 21–36*, 606–7).

6. Possibly a superstitious custom of foreign origin. There is a belief in many cultures, ancient and modern, that it is unlucky to step upon a threshold (Driver). See 1 Sam 5:4–5.

*And howling from the Second Quarter*[7]
   *and a loud crash from the hills*
[11]*Howl, inhabitants of the Mortar!*[8]
   *for all the people of Canaan*[9] *have ceased to be*
      *all those laden with silver are cut off*

[12]*And it will be at that time*
   *I will search Jerusalem with lamps*
      *and I will visit the men*
*Who are thickening upon their lees*[10]
   *those who say in their hearts*
*"Yahweh will not do good*
   *nor will he do evil"*
[13]*And it will be their wealth will become plunder*
   *and their houses a waste*
*Yes, they will build houses*
   *but they will not inhabit them*
*And they will plant vineyards*
   *but they will not drink wine from them*
[14]*The great day of Yahweh is at hand*
   *at hand, and much hastening*
*The sound of the day of Yahweh!*
   *the warrior cries there bitterly*
[15]*A day of wrath is that day*
   *a day of distress and stress*
*A day of ruin and desolation*
   *a day of darkness and gloom*

---

7. The place in Jerusalem where the prophetess Huldah resided (2 Kgs 22:14).

8. The Mortar (a hollowed-out "pounding place"; cf. Prov 27:22; Judg 15:19) was evidently a part of Jerusalem where traders dwelt (Driver).

9. Traders residing in Judah.

10. An expression taken from wine, here perhaps meaning "easygoing men sunk in a state of moral stagnation and spiritual indifference" (Driver).

*A day of clouds and thick clouds*
 *[16]a day of trumpet blast and battle cry*
*Against the fortified cities*
 *and against the lofty battlements*[11]

*[17]I will bring distress to humanity*
 *so that they walk like the blind*
  *because they have sinned against Yahweh*
*And their blood will be poured out like dust*
 *and their flesh like dung*

*[18]Neither their silver nor their gold*
 *will be able to deliver them*
  *in the day of Yahweh's fury*
*And in the fire of his jealousy*
 *all the earth will be consumed*
*For an end, surely a terrible one he will make*
 *of all the inhabitants of the earth.*

RHETORIC AND COMPOSITION

The present passage is delimited in the Hebrew Bible by a section after 1:18, which is also the end of the chapter. Another section comes at the end of 1:9, which may indicate that two prophecies have been combined into one. The passage has an overarching theme: an all-consuming day of Yahweh awaits Jerusalem and Judah for its idolatry, violence, and fraud.

Smith[12] says Zephaniah pales in comparison to Jeremiah. He cannot be considered a great poet possessing great imaginative powers, deep insight into the human

---

11. These were elevated corners of ancient walled cities, apparently with battlements, manned by defenders in wartime (Zeph 3:6; cf. Jer 31:38, 40; 2 Chr 26:15),

12. Smith, "Zephaniah," 176, 178.

heart, or keen sensitivity to these beauties of nature. He also lacks sympathy, compassion, or emotion over the fate of his people that so pervades the utterances of Jeremiah. While it may be true that Zephaniah does not have the deep insight into the human heart that Jeremiah does, nor does he give us personal confessions such as the great prophet of Anathoth does, Berlin says he nevertheless shows considerable ability as a poet.

There are a number of striking repetitions in the poetry of Zephaniah. Muilenburg[13] said Hebrew rhetoric had a proclivity to strive after totality, and it can be seen no better than in the present passage. In 1:2–6 is repetition with anaphora at beginning and end:

1:2–5   *I will utterly sweep away* everything
          *from upon the face of the earth, oracle of Yahweh*
          *I will sweep away humans* and beasts;
          *I will sweep away* birds of the heavens and fish of the sea
          . . . . . . . . . .
          And I will cut off *humans*
              *from upon the face of the earth, oracle of Yahweh*
          . . . . . . . . . . . .
          *And those who bow down* upon the roofs to the host of heaven
              *and those who bow down, who swear* to Yahweh
                  *and who swear* by Milcom

1:8–10  *And it will be on the day . . .*
              *that I will visit . . .*
          *And I will visit . . .*
              *on that day*
          *And it will be on that day . . .*

13. Muilenburg, "Study in Hebrew Rhetoric," 99.

In 1:14–16a is more repetition with a series of hendiadys:

1:14–16a  *The great day of Yahweh is at hand*
     *at hand*, and much hastening
  The sound of *the day of Yahweh*!
     the warrior cries there bitterly
  *A day* of wrath is *that day*
     *a day of distress and stress*
  *A day of ruin and desolation*
     *a day of darkness and gloom*
  *A day of clouds and thick clouds*
     *a day of trumpet blast and battle cry*

In 1:15 is alliteration in the Hebrew:

*A day of ruin and desolation*

One of the difficulties in the present passage is knowing who is speaking: Yahweh or Zephaniah? Yahweh is clearly the speaking voice at the beginning, but at 1:7 it sounds as if Zephaniah is the one calling people to be silent before Lord Yahweh. Then in 1:8–11 it is Yahweh again, saying that he will be meting out a punishment resulting in loud sounds of wailing. In 1:12 it appears again to be Zephaniah, saying he will search Jerusalem with lamps, although Driver and others think Yahweh will be doing the search. All of 1:12–18 could well be the voice of Zephaniah, although in 1:17 Yahweh is saying that he will bring distress upon the people. What we may also have in this discourse is a prophet identifying so completely with Yahweh that he does not distinguish between Yahweh's voice and his own. Things are usually clearer with Jeremiah (cf. Jer 5:1–9). In Deuteronomy one will note that Moses occasionally assumes the voice of Yahweh where otherwise he himself is always the speaker (Deut 7:4; 11:14–15; 17:3; 28:20, 68; 29:5–6).

## MESSAGE

The present passage is Zephaniah's great prophecy on the day of Yahweh, building and expanding as it does upon Amos's dire word to Northern Israelites in Amos 5:18–20. Amos transformed an earlier idea, saying that Yahweh now had judgment in view for Samaria and Northern Israel. Isaiah saw a day of Yahweh slated for the Babylonians (Isa 13:6), but Zephaniah sees the ominous day for Jerusalem and all Judah. Jeremiah preached the same message (Jer 4:9; 12:3; 17:16; 30:7). In earlier times, Israel awaited a day of Yahweh when in holy war Yahweh would lead his people in a defeat of their enemies.[14] But now holy war is being declared upon Judah. Jeremiah, too, saw a holy war being waged against Judah (Jer 6:4–5).[15]

Worship of Canaanite and Phoenician Baals,[16] along with gods of Assyria and other nations, presided over by idolatrous priests who had people bowing down to them, caused people to turn away from Yahweh and no longer seek him in prayers and acts of worship (cf. Jer 2:23; 7:9). Those responsible for this sorry state of affairs, says Yahweh, will be punished. Zephaniah appears to have provided impetus for Josiah's purge of idolatrous worship in the reform this good king carried out (Driver). The prophet was a contemporary of Jeremiah, perhaps an older contemporary, as Jeremiah's earliest preaching has much the same message

14. Von Rad, "Origin of the Concept of the Day of Yahweh."

15. Lundbom, *Jeremiah 1–20*, 418.

16. Baal is properly the "owner" of a particular region; thus the existence of numerous local Baal gods—Baal of Peor (Deut 4:3), Baal-zebul of Ekron (2 Kgs 1:2), etc.

(Jer 2–3). Both prophets after railing against idolatry called people to repent (Zeph 2:1–15; Jer 4:1–4).

Zephaniah begins the present prophecy with Yahweh saying that he is about to sweep away everything—humans, beasts, birds overhead, and fish in the sea from the face of the earth. A rather comprehensive act of divine destruction, but Jeremiah in his vision envisioned a return to primeval chaos (Jer 4:23–26). The expression "from the face of the earth" occurs in the Flood story (Gen 6:7; 7:4; 8:8). The Flood story also promises a destruction of humans, animals, creeping things, and birds of the air (Gen 6:7), but not fish of the sea. Hosea's word of judgment mourns the loss of fish (Hos 4:3), and in Ezekiel's future day of Yahweh's wrath fish of the sea will be affected (Ezek 38:19–20).

This sweeping will take in Jerusalem and all Judah, then certain individuals inhabiting them. See Hosea's judgment on Northern Israel in Hos 4:1–3. Yahweh will do away with stumbling blocks and the wicked associated with them. Remnants of Baal worship along with foreign and local priests of Baal will be cut off. The foreign (Chemarim) priests, which Hosea observed in Northern Israel (Hos 10:5), were cut off by Josiah in his Judah reform (2 Kgs 23:5). The practice of bowing down on rooftops to the host of heaven, brought into Judah by Manasseh (2 Kgs 21:3, 5), must also, says Yahweh, come to an end (Jer 8:2; 19:13; 32:29; cf. Deut 4:19; 17:3). Josiah did away with rooftop worship in his reform (2 Kgs 23:12). Yahweh observed people bowing down to him and at the same time swearing by the Ammonite god Milcom, a syncretism he would not tolerate (cf. Deut 6:13; 10:20). All of this constituted a turning away from Yahweh, not seeking him where "seeking" would mean seeking Yahweh in prayer and acts of worship (2 Sam 12:16; 21:1). "Inquiring" could mean going to Yahweh or a prophet for an oracle (Gen 25:22–23; Exod 18:15;

1 Kgs 14:5; 22:5–8). The two terms, "seeking" and "inquiring," often occur together (cf. Deut 4:29; Jer 29:13; Pss 24:6; 105:3–4).

The prophet becomes the speaking voice in 1:7. Zephaniah admonishes people to keep silent before Lord Yahweh (cf. Hab 2:20; Zech 2:13 [Heb 2:17]), for the day of Yahweh is at hand (Isa 13:6; Ezek 30:3; Obad 15; Joel 1:15; 3:14). Yahweh on this day will have prepared a sacrifice, consecrated invited guests, and made an unwelcomed visit to the king's sons, court officials, and all who are dressed in foreign attire. Judah will be the sacrificial victim; invited guests will be Judah's enemies (cf. Jer 46:10; Ezek 39:17). But who are the king's sons? Josiah was still a minor at the time he came to the Jerusalem throne (2 Kgs 22:1), so if this prophecy is dated early in his reign, reference cannot be to any of his sons. Reference also cannot have been to Josiah himself, for neither Zephaniah nor Jeremiah saw any wrongdoing in Josiah. If the prophecy is dated later in Josiah's reign, Zephaniah could have known the young Jehoahaz before he became king. He was a son of Josiah (2 Kgs 23:30) and is given a bad obituary by the Deuteronomic Historian (2 Kgs 23:32). Zephaniah could also have known Eliakim/Jehoiakim before he became king. He, too, was a son of Josiah (2 Kgs 23:34) and is given a bad obituary by the Deuteronomic Historian and the Chronicler (2 Kgs 24:37; 2 Chr 36:5). Driver points out that Josiah's two sons, Jehoiakim and Jehoahaz, would in the king's eighteenth year (622) have been not more than twelve and ten years old respectively (2 Kgs 23:31, 36). Jeremiah had no use for Jehoiakim after he became king, and predicted for him a shameful death (Jer 22:13–19). Officials cited by Zephaniah were probably some serving under Josiah (Jer 4:9). Zephaniah also depreciates those dressed in foreign apparel, who could have been worshipers of Baal (2 Kgs 10:22) or court officials assuming foreign dress (Driver). Jeremiah had no use for those carrying on diplomatic relations with Egypt and Assyria (Jer 2:18).

Yahweh will "visit" for purposes of punishment (Jer 9:25 [Heb 9:24]; 11:22; 13:21) those who practice superstitious customs of the day (cf. 1 Sam 5:5), and also more ordinary people who fill their master's house with violence and deceit. Jeremiah found in his search of Jerusalem that the poor were no less guilty of breaking Yahweh's yoke than the great (Jer 5:4–5). Driver (citing Smith) thinks reference could be foreign bodyguards of Judahite kings, "who were addicted to corruption and intrigue." The "master's house" has been taken by some to be the temple (Berlin).

On the day of Yahweh, howlings, loud cries, and deafening sounds will be heard in every quarter of Jerusalem—at the Fish Gate on the northern wall (Neh 3:3; 12:39; 2 Chr 33:14), in the Second Quarter (2 Kgs 22:14), in the Mortar where Canaanite/Phoenician merchants did their trading (Isa 23:8; Neh 13:16), and on Jerusalem's surrounding hills. Canaanite merchants and those having weighed out silver in quantity will be gone.

Zephaniah will search the dark corners of Jerusalem with lamps,[17] making unwelcomed visits to morally and decadent individuals who say, "Yahweh will not do good, nor will he do evil"—i.e., he will do nothing at all (cf. Jer 10:5 and Isa 41:23–24 on idols). John Singer Sargent's *Frieze of the Prophets*, in the Boston Public Library, has Zephaniah holding a lamp in his left hand. Jeremiah, along with others, searched the streets of Jerusalem to find just one person who acted justly and sought truth, but he turned up no one (Jer 5:1–9). Some 250 years later it was the Cynic Diogenes

---

17. Other commentators, beginning with Driver, think Yahweh is the one who will be searching Jerusalem with lamps. But Yahweh is referred to in the third person at the conclusion of the verse.

who lit a lamp in broad daylight and walked the streets of Athens "looking for [an honest] man."

In 1:13 Zephaniah says the wealth of Jerusalem's merchants will become plunder, their houses a waste. All their labor will be for nought. They may build houses, but they will not live in them (cf. Amos 5:11; contrast Isa 65:21). They may plant vineyards, but they will not drink wine from the grapes (cf. Mic 6:15). Both were curses in Deuteronomy for those in violation of the Horeb/Sinai covenant (Deut 28:30, 39).

Zephaniah then describes in more detail the great day of Yahweh announced in 1:7. It is coming with all haste. Warriors, whose job it is to defend the city, will be crying bitter tears on that day (Amos 2:14–16). The day will be one of distress, ruin, and destruction; of darkness and gloom; of thick clouds, of trumpet blasts and cries from those forced into battle. Portents in the sky—darkness, gloom, and thick clouds—carry overtones of calamity here as elsewhere in the Bible, and prophets predict distress in similar terms (Amos 5:18–20; 8:9; Isa 8:22; 13:10; Jer 13:16; Ezek 34:12; Joel 2:2, 10, 30–31). Trumpet blasts and shouts accompanying them are the sounds of war (Amos 1:14; 2:2). Zephaniah says the distress will be felt by everyone in Judah's fortified cities and lofty battlements—so much so that they will walk about like those who are blind. The blind at such times have little chance of escape (cf. Deut 28:28–29; Isa 59:9–10). All this will come about because people have sinned against Yahweh. Blood will be spilled, and flesh will be as dung. All the silver and gold will not be able to deliver people on this day of Yahweh's jealous fury (cf. Ezek 7:19). Yahweh is "a devouring fire, a jealous God" (Deut 4:24; Ps 79:5; cf. Nah 1:2). The entire earth will be consumed. Yahweh is going to bring a terrible end to everyone and everything.

## REFLECTION

1. Do we need to be watchful about a "Day of the Lord" such as Zephaniah saw coming in his time? How might Zephaniah's "Day of the Lord" prophecy affect New Testament teachings such as Matt 11:20–24; 24:1–51; 1 Thess 5:1–10; 2 Thess 2:1–12; and 2 Pet 3:1–13?

2. What sort of idols do people bow down to in our day? Do such turn people away from the Lord and cause them to no longer seek him?

3. What sort of reform is needed today in America? Can voices raised by ordinary people bring change at the highest levels of government? Might repentance also figure in?

4. What are some of the superstitious customs of our day? Are they harmless, or do they impede genuine faith?

# 4

# "SEEK YAHWEH, YOU HUMBLE OF THE LAND" (2:1-15)

2 ¹*Gather yourselves together, yes gather*
   *O nation having no shame*
 ²*Before the decree goes forth*
   *like chaff vanishing in a day*
 *Before it surely comes upon you*
   *the fierce anger of Yahweh*
 *Before it surely comes upon you*
   *the day of Yahweh's anger*
 ³*Seek Yahweh, all you humble of the land*
   *who have done his ordinance*
 *Seek righteousness, seek humility*
   *perhaps you may be hidden*
     *on the day of Yahweh's anger*
 ⁴*For Gaza will be deserted*
   *and Ashkelon become a waste*
 *Ashdod they will drive out at noon*
   *and Ekron will be uprooted*

⁵Woe to inhabitants of the seacoast
  nation of the Cherethites![1]
The word of Yahweh is against you
  O Canaan, land of the Philistines
    and I will destroy you without inhabitant

⁶And the seacoast will become pastures
  encampments for shepherds
    and folds for flocks
⁷The region will be for the remnant of the house of Judah
  upon which they will pasture
In houses of Ashkelon
  they will lie down at evening
For Yahweh their God will visit them
  and restore their fortunes

⁸I have heard the taunts of Moab
  and the revilings of the Ammonites
How they taunted my people
  and magnified themselves over their border
⁹Therefore as I live, oracle of Yahweh of hosts, God of Israel
Indeed Moab will become like Sodom
  and the Ammonites like Gomorrah
A place possessed by weeds and salt pits
  and a waste forever
The remnant of my people will plunder them
  and survivors of my nation will possess them

¹⁰This they will have for their pride
  because they taunted and magnified themselves
    over the people of Yahweh of hosts
¹¹Yahweh will be awesome over them
  indeed, he makes lean all the gods of the earth
And to him will bow down
  each from its own place
    all the islands of the nations

---

1. Most probably a clan of the Philistines who immigrated from Caphtor (Crete); cf. Amos 9:7.

*Seek Yahweh, You Humble of the Land*

*¹²You also, O Cushites²*
  *will be slain by my sword*

*¹³And he will stretch out his hand against the north*
  *and he will destroy Ashur*
*And he will make Nineveh a waste*
  *a dry land like the desert*
*¹⁴And flocks will lie down in the midst of it*
  *all species of beasts*
*Also the pelican, also the porcupine*
  *will lodge on its capitals³*
*A sound of one singing in the window*
  *desolation in the thresholds*
    *indeed its cedar work he has laid bare*
*¹⁵This is the exultant city*
  *that dwelt secure*
*That said in its heart*
  *"I am and there is no one else"*
*What a waste it has become*
  *a lair for wild beasts!*
*Everyone who passes by it*
  *hisses and shakes his fist.*


## RHETORIC AND COMPOSITION

This passage is delimited by section markings before 2:1 and after 2:15, which are also the chapter limits. Another section after 2:4 could indicate that 2:1–4 was once a separate prophecy (Berlin). The messenger formula in 2:10 may indicate the beginning of yet another prophecy, but more likely it is the center of a larger passage. Oracle formulas are

---

2. I.e., dark-skinned Ethiopians living south of Egypt (cf. Jer 13:23; Nah 3:9).

3. The carved decorated tops of pillars (1 Kgs 7:16–17; Amos 9:1), which now lie broken on the ground.

not inserted at random in prophetic oracles (*pace* Roberts);[4] they appear at the beginning (Zeph 1:2, 3; 3:8; Jer 2:29; 3:1, 12, 14, 16; 4:1), more often at the end (Nah 2:13 [Heb 2:14]; Zeph 3:20; Jer 2:3, 9, 19, 22; 3:10, 13, 20; 4:9), and occasionally in the middle (Zeph 1:10; 2:9; Nah 3:5; Jer 1:7; 2:12). The present passage has an overarching theme, which is that Yahweh has an unwelcomed day of judgment in store for the nations (2:4–15), and Judah, if it seeks Yahweh, may perhaps be hidden from Yahweh's day of wrath (2:1–3).

The passage changes from speaker to speaker without warning:

| 2:1–4 | Zephaniah speaks |
| 2:5 | Yahweh speaks |
| 2:6–7 | Zephaniah speaks |
| 2:8–9 | Yahweh speaks |
| 2:10–11 | Zephaniah speaks |
| 2:12 | Yahweh speaks |
| 2:13–15 | Zephaniah speaks |

Zephaniah is again seen to be fond of repetition and balanced terms. In the first three verses are these repetitions:

> 2:1 *Gather yourselves together, yes gather together*
> 2:2 *Before* the decree goes forth . . .
> *Before it surely comes upon you* . . .
> *Before it surely comes upon you* . . .
> 2:3 *Seek* Yahweh . . .
> *Seek* righteousness, *seek* humility . . .

In the Hebrew are also two paronomasias (wordplays in sound):

> 2:4 *For Gaza will be deserted*
> . . . . . . . . . . . . . . . . . .
> *and Ekron will be uprooted*

---

4. Roberts, *Zephaniah*, 170.

## MESSAGE

Zephaniah begins this oracle by calling people of a shameless nation to gather together in self-examination before a decree goes forth, before Yahweh's fierce anger comes upon them. That nation is doubtless Judah, and the call is to repentance. Zephaniah is echoing Amos's preaching to Northern Israel. The humble are told to seek Yahweh and do his ordinances (cf. Amos 5:6–7; Jer 8:7b; Isa 55:6; 58:2), to seek righteousness and humility (cf. Amos 5:14; Mic 6:8) before it is too late. Perhaps they may be hidden on the day of Yahweh's anger, but just perhaps (cf. Amos 5:15b; Isa 26:20). Jeremiah, too, preached the possibility of avoiding Yahweh's wrath if people amended their ways and their doings (Jer 7:3–7; 26:3; 36:3).

Judahites are warned because judgment is coming upon four cities of the Philistine pentapolis. Gath was no more (Amos 9:7; Jer 25:20), having been conquered by Sargon II when he took Ashdod in 711 ($ANET^3$ 286; cf. Amos 6:2; Isa 20). Ashdod will now be surprised with an attack at noonday when people are at rest (2 Sam 4:5; 1 Kgs 20:16; cf. Jer 6:4a; 15:8).

Yahweh confirms the word of the prophet, declaring woe upon inhabitants of the seacoast: first upon the Cherethites (1 Sam 30:14; Ezek 25:16), a clan of Philistines that emigrated from Caphtor/Crete (Deut 2:23; Amos 9:7; Jer 47:4); then upon Canaan, reckoned as Philistine territory in Num 13:29; Josh 13:3. He will destroy these people so they are without inhabitant. The expression "without inhabitant," occurring again in 3:6, is used often by Jeremiah (Jer 4:7, 29; 9:11 [Heb 9:10]; 26:9; 34:22; 46:19; 48:9; 51:29). Zephaniah continues the judgment on the seacoast, saying it will become pastures, encampments for shepherds, and folds for flocks (cf. Amos 1:2). The remnant of Judah will possess the region when Yahweh restores its fortunes, and they will be the ones pasturing there (Isa 11:14; Jer 49:2; Obad 19-20). Return from an earlier exile is assumed. Jeremiah in his early preaching looked for a return of exiles from the north country (Jer 31:1-20). At that time returnees will lie down in houses of Ashkelon at evening. Yahweh will "visit" his people for good (cf. Jer 27:22; 29:10), and restore their fortunes.

Yahweh is again the speaker in 2:8-9. He recalls taunts of the Moabites (cf. Ezek 25:8-11) and the Ammonites against his people. Ammonites sought to enlarge their border with Israel (Amos 1:13; Jer 49:1). Both peoples taunted Judah again when Jerusalem fell in 587/6, and were rebuked by Yahweh (Ezek 21:28-32; 25:3-7, 8-11). Yahweh now swears by himself (cf. Heb 6:13) that Moab will be as Sodom and the Ammonites as Gomorrah—places of weeds and salt pits (Gen 18:16—19:29). Sodom and Gomorrah (with Admah and Zeboiim) became proverbial among Biblical writers as decadent cities punished for their gross wickedness (Deut 29:23 [Heb 29:22]; 32:32; Amos 4:11; Isa 1:9-10; 13:19; Jer 23:14; 49:18; 50:40; Matt 10:15; 2 Pet 2:6; etc.). Judah's remnant will plunder Moab and the Ammonites.

Zephaniah returns as speaker in 2:10-11, saying that plundering Moab and the Ammonites will be a reward for their pride (cf. Prov 16:18), for taunting and magnifying themselves over Yahweh's people (Isa 16:6; Jer 48:26, 29-30). Yahweh will be awesome over them, making lean their gods and all other gods; i.e., Yahweh will deprive these gods of their sacrificial offerings. But bowing down to Yahweh will be inhabitants of islands to the west (cf. Mic 4:1-4).

Yahweh is the speaker in 2:12, saying that as for Ethiopians to the south, they will be slain by his sword. Zephaniah finishes the oracle as speaker in 2:13-15, looking climactically to the north and saying that Yahweh's wrath will be poured out against the city of Ashur. Ashur can also be rendered Assyria, but the former is preferable because of the balancing with Nineveh. Ashur, the ancient capital of Assyria, was destroyed by Cyaxares and the Medes a couple years before the destruction of Nineveh. The great city of Nineveh will become a desert with birds and domestic and wild animals inhabiting the ruins. A devastating judgment for a city on the banks of Tigris! Birds, oblivious to the desolation, will sing in open windows and in the thresholds. Mention of thresholds with capitals in the previous line is an attempt by the prophet to portray ruined buildings from top to bottom. Nineveh's beautiful cedarwork will lie in ruins. The proud city that thought it was like no other will be a desert and home to wild animals. All who pass by will hiss and shake their fists (cf. Nah 3:19; Jer 18:16; 50:13; Lam 2:15). This prophecy anticipates Nineveh's fall in 612. The earlier prophecy anticipates Nebuchadnezzar's arrival in the Philistine Plain at which time Ashkelon was destroyed in 604 and Ekron in 603.

## REFLECTION

1. We are accustomed to hearing preached that it is God who *finds us* in our sin and need, like the shepherd in Jesus's parable who leaves the ninety-nine and goes out and find the sheep that is lost (Luke 15:3–7). But should we not also *seek* God? See Amos 5:6; Isa 55:6; and Matt 7:7–11.

2. Do we not assume that if we humble ourselves God will certainly spare us calamity? Why then does Zephaniah (and also Amos) say "perhaps"?

3. Zephaniah and Nahum both anticipate the fall of Assyria. Why do you think Jeremiah says not a word about this huge event occurring on the world scene?

4. Is there not a danger of any nation—including the United States—thinking that "I am and there is no one else"?

# 5

# "WOE TO THE DEFIANT, DEFILED, AND OPPRESSING CITY" (3:1-7)

3 ¹Woe to her that is defiant and defiled
  the oppressing city!
²She listens to no voice
  she takes no correction
She trusts not in Yahweh
  she does not draw near to her God
³Her officials within her
  are roaring lions
Her judges are evening wolves
  that leave nothing till the morning
⁴Her prophets are reckless
  treacherous men
Her priests profane what is sacred
  they do violence to the law
⁵Yahweh within her is righteous
  he does no wrong

*Morning by morning he gives his justice to light*
　*it does not fail*
　　*but the unjust knows no shame*

*⁶I have cut off nations*
　*their battlements are in ruins*
*I have made desolate their streets*
　*without any walking in them*
*Their cities have been laid waste*
　*not a person, without inhabitant*
*⁷I said, "Surely you will fear me*
　*you will accept correction*
*and it will not be cut off from her eyes*[1]
　*all that I have laid upon her"*
*But they rose early to corrupt*
　*all their deeds.*

## RHETORIC AND COMPOSITION

This passage is delimited at the top by a section in the Hebrew Bible before 3:1. The lower limit is determined by the "oracle of Yahweh" formula beginning 3:8. Driver and Smith both take 3:1–7 as a unit. The theme of 3:1–7 is a soiled, defiled Jerusalem that listens to no one.

There is this change in speaker in the passage:

　　3:1–5　Zephaniah speaks
　　3:6–7　Yahweh speaks

In 3:5 is a repetition picking up on the term in 3:3:

　　⁵Morning by morning

In 3:3 and 3:5 is this repetition:

　　³Her officials *within her* are roaring lions
　　⁵Yahweh *within her* is righteous

---

1. Reading with the LXX; MT has "her dwelling."

In 3:6 is this repetition:

> ⁶I have made desolate their streets
>    *without* any walking in them
> Their cities have been laid waste
>    *without* a person, no inhabitant

## MESSAGE

Zephaniah in this passage is crying out against Jerusalem, a city defiant, defiled, and filled with oppression (cf. Isa 30:9; Jer 5:1–9). She listens to no one, takes no correction, and puts no trust in Yahweh (Jer 4:17; 5:23; Ezek 5:6). The expressions "listens to no voice" and "takes no correction" are favorites of Jeremiah. He called people to listen to / obey Yahweh's voice (Jer 11:4), but says they failed to do so (Jer 7:23–26; 11:7–8; 22:21), and he called them to accept correction (35:13), but says they refused to accept it (Jer 2:30; 5:3; 7:28; 17:23; 32:33). "Correction" is a wisdom term, occurring some thirty times in the Proverbs (Prov 1:2–3, 7–8; 3:11; 4:1, 13; 5:12, 23; etc.).

Judah's officials (princes), judges, prophets, and priests are all unworthy of their offices. Officials and judges are guilty of taking people's assets like wild animals consuming prey, leaving nothing until morning (Isa 1:23; Mic 3:11; Ezek 22:25 [LXX], 27). A judgment on the upper classes who exploit the poor and less fortunate (Isa 1:23; 3:14; 5:8–10, 23; 10:2; Mic 2:2; 3:1–3, 9; Prov 28:14; cf. Jer 7:6; 22:3). Prophets are reckless, treacherous men (Mic 3:6–7), where "reckless" can mean giving false prophesies (Mic 2:11; Jer 23:32; cf. Ezek 23:28; cf. Jer 14:13–14; 23:16–17) and "treacherous" can mean "being faithless." Priests profane what is sacred (cf. Lev 10:10) and do violence to Yahweh's law (Hos 4:6—5:1; 6:9; Mic 3:11; Isa 28:7; Hab 1:4; Ezek

22:26; cf. Deut 17:8–12; 21:5). Priests are supposed to be custodians of the law (Jer 18:18; Ezek 7:26; cf. Deut 33:10), but Jeremiah said those who handle the law do not know Yahweh (Jer 2:8). Jeremiah knew of treacherous priests even within his own household (Jer 12:6). Prophets were prophesying falsely and priests were ruling at their direction (Jer 5:30–31; 6:13; 14:18b). He asked Yahweh why such people were allowed to thrive (Jer 12:1).

Yahweh, by contrast, is righteous, says Zephaniah, doing no wrong (Deut 32:4; Jer 12:1; cf. Exod 9:27). Morning by morning his justice shines forth brightly (Hos 6:5; Ps 37:6); it does not fail. On the idiom "morning by morning," see GKC §123d. But the unjust knows no shame. Morning is the time when court convenes and justice is expected to go forth (Jer 21:12; Ps 101:8; Ruth 3:14—4:12).

Yahweh says he has cut off nations; their battlements lie in ruins (cf. 1:16). No one can be seen walking their streets; entire cities have been laid waste (Jer 2:15; 4:7; 9:11–12 [Heb 9:10–11]; 33:10]). Yahweh hoped the people of Jerusalem would fear/revere him (cf. Ps 11:10; Prov 1:7; 9:10), that they would accept correction, but it was a vain hope. Instead, people rose early to do corrupt deeds. The expression "rose early" appearing with another verb emphasizes that verb (GKC §113k); it occurs ten times in Jeremiah's prose (Jer 7:13, 25; 11:7; 25:3, 4; 29:19; 32:33; 35:14, 15; 44:4) and is a signature phrase of the prophet. See also 2 Chr 36:15. People of Jerusalem "rising early" to do evil deeds contrasts with Yahweh executing justice "morning by morning."

REFLECTION

1. Are whole cities today "defiant, defiled, and filled with oppression"? Perhaps the prophet is given to

exaggeration. Might there not have been some who were upright?

2. What about judges in our modern cities? Can we trust them to execute justice?

3. Do you ever wonder why God allows treacherous people to thrive? Will it go on indefinitely? How do you handle these questions in your prayer life?

4. Do you know people today who are without shame? How do you handle them, or can you handle them?

# 6

# "THEREFORE WAIT FOR ME, ORACLE OF YAHWEH" (3:8-20)

3 ⁸*Therefore wait for me, oracle of Yahweh*
   *for the day when I arise to the prey*
*Indeed my decision is to gather nations*
   *to assemble kingdoms*
*To pour out upon them my judgment*
   *all my fierce anger*
*Indeed in the fire of my jealousy*
   *all the earth will be consumed*
⁹*Indeed then I will turn unto the peoples*
   *a purified speech*
*To all of them calling on the name of Yahweh*
   *to serving him with one accord*
¹⁰*From beyond the rivers of Cush*[1]
   *my worshipers, daughter of my dispersed ones*
     *will bear my offering*
¹¹*In that day you will not be put to shame*

---

1. I.e., Ethiopia.

*Therefore Wait for Me, Oracle of Yahweh*

*for all your doings*
   *which you rebelled against me*
*Indeed then I will remove from your midst*
   *your proudly exultant ones*
*And you will no longer be haughty*
   *on my holy mountain*
¹²*Yes I will leave in your midst*
   *a people humble and poor*
      *and they will seek refuge in the name of Yahweh*
¹³*The remnant of Israel*
   *will not do wrong*
      *and will not speak a lie*
*And there will not be found in their mouth*
   *a deceitful tongue*
*Indeed they will pasture and lie down*
   *and none will make them afraid*

¹⁴*Sing O daughter of Zion*
   *shout O Israel!*
*Rejoice and exult with all the heart*
   *O daughter of Jerusalem!*
¹⁵*Yahweh has taken away your judgments*
   *he has cast out your enemies*
*The King of Israel, Yahweh, is in your midst*
   *you will fear evil no more*
¹⁶*In that day it will be said to Jerusalem*
   "*Do not fear O Zion*
      *let not your hands grow weak*
¹⁷*Yahweh, your God, is in your midst*
   *the Mighty One who gives salvation*"
*He will rejoice over you with joy*
   *he will quietly renew you in his love*
      *he will rejoice over you with loud singing*

¹⁸*I will gather the grieved from the appointed feast*
   *they will be from you*
      *upon whom reproach was a burden*

> [19] *Behold I will deal with all who oppress you*
>    *at that time*
> *And I will save those who limp*
>    *and the banished ones I will assemble*
> *And I will make them a praise and a name*
>    *whose shame has been in all the earth*
> [20] *At that time I will bring you in*
>    *and at that time I will gather you*
> *Indeed I will make you a name and a praise*
>    *among all peoples of the earth*
> *When I restore your fortunes*
>    *before your eyes, said Yahweh.*

## RHETORIC AND COMPOSITION

This unit is delimited by oracle formulas in 3:8 and 3:20. Verse 20 is the end of the book. In the Hebrew Bible there is also a section marking after 3:13, which could indicate two hope passages combined into one. The passage contains a change of speaker:

| | |
|---|---|
| 3:8–13 | Yahweh is the speaker |
| 3:14–17 | Zephaniah is the speaker |
| 3:18–20 | Yahweh is the speaker |

Yahweh tells the faithful in Jerusalem to wait for him until judgment is complete; then Zephaniah tells Jerusalem to sing and rejoice because Yahweh has taken away the judgment against it, and Yahweh is in its midst; then Yahweh says he will deal with Jerusalem's oppressors, bring back those who are in exile, and restore her fortunes.

Zephaniah's poetry continues to have impressive repetition. Six lines begin with an asseverative *kî*, "indeed":

> [8] *Indeed my decision is to gather nations . . .*
> [8] *Indeed in the fire of my jealousy . . .*
> [9] *Indeed then I will turn unto the peoples . . .*

*Therefore Wait for Me, Oracle of Yahweh*

<sup>11</sup>*Indeed* then I will remove from your midst . . .
<sup>13</sup>*Indeed* they will pasture and lie down . . .
<sup>20</sup>*Indeed* I will make you a name and a praise . . .

One will also note the following repetitions:

<sup>11</sup>. . . *from your midst*
<sup>12</sup>. . . *in your midst*
<sup>15</sup>. . . *in your midst*
<sup>17</sup>. . . *in your midst*

Twice in the passage is this repetition:

<sup>11</sup>*In that day* . . .
<sup>16</sup>*In that day* . . .

The prophet and Yahweh repeat a similar expression:

<sup>19</sup>*at that time* . . .
<sup>20</sup>*At that time* . . .
<sup>20</sup>*and at that time* . . .

Yahweh's concluding oracle has these repetitions:

<sup>19</sup>*And I will make them a praise and a name*
   whose shame has been *in all the earth*
<sup>20</sup>*At that time* I will bring you in
   *and at that time* I will gather you
*Indeed I will make you a name and a praise*
   *among all peoples of the earth*

## MESSAGE

After Zephaniah's ringing rebuke of an oppressive Jerusalem whose officials, judges, prophets, and priests are all guilty of wrongdoing, he follows with an oracle in which Yahweh says "wait for me," a theme heard often in Isaiah (Isa 8:17; 26:8; 30:18; 33:2; 64:4; cf. 2 Kgs 19), in the Psalms (Pss 23:3, 5, 21; 27:14; 31:24; etc.), by Zephaniah's contemporary,

Habakkuk (Hab 2:3), and elsewhere (Lam 3:25-26). Yahweh will arise to address the prey (i.e., his oppressed covenant people), for he has decided to gather the nations and pour out his wrath upon them (Jer 25:31, 33; Joel 3:11-16). Judgment is not against the wicked rulers of Jerusalem (*pace* Roberts). Then, wonder of wonders, Yahweh will turn the speech of the nations into a pure speech so all will call upon his name and serve him only (2:11; cf. Isa 6:5-7). The nations' impure speech was praying and swearing by other gods (Hos 2:16-17 [Heb 2:18-19]). From beyond the rivers of distant Ethiopia exiles will return home bearing offerings in procession (cf. Isa 11:11; 18:1-2, 7; Pss 68:29 [Heb 68:30]; 76:11 [Heb 76:12]).

In that day, says Yahweh, something wonderful will happen to you, O Judah. You will not be shamed as in the past because of your rebellions against me (Ezek 39:26), for I will remove all the proud and haughty among you so they will no longer be found on Zion, my holy mountain (Isa 1:25-27; 4:3; 10:22). What I will do, says Yahweh, is to leave in your midst a people humble and lowly who will seek refuge in my name (2:3; Isa 14:32; 25:4; 29:19; Nah 1:7; Pss 12:5 [Heb 12:6]; 18:27 [Heb 18:28]; 35:10; 118:8-9). This remnant of my chosen people will do no wrong and speak no lie (cf. Jer 31:33-34). Their tongues will be cleansed of all deceit. I will make them eat and lie down as sheep in a peaceful pasture where none will make them afraid (cf. Mic 2:12; 4:4; 7:14; Isa 14:30; Ezek 34:11-15).

In the concluding verses both the prophet and Yahweh sing with joy over future days. Zephaniah in 3:14 is now the speaking voice, telling people to sing loudly and shout, to rejoice with all their heart, for Yahweh has taken away the judgments against her (cf. Isa 49:13; 54:1). Her enemies have been dealt with. Verbs here are prophetic perfects. Yahweh, King of Israel, is in their midst (Num 14:14; Isa

12:6; Jer 14:9; Joel 2:27). People will fear evil no more. In that day Zion's people need have no fear, their hands will not grow weak in fear, for Yahweh, their God, will be in their midst. Yahweh, the Mighty One, is the one who brings salvation. On Yahweh as the "Mighty One" or "Warrior" bringing salvation, see Isa 9:6 [Heb 9:5]; 42:13; Jer 14:9; 20:11. Yahweh will rejoice over his people with joy (Jer 32:41; Isa 62:5; 65:19), will quietly renew them in his love, and will rejoice with loud singing.

The first line of 3:18 is difficult. Yahweh, now the speaking voice, says something about gathering from among his people those who grieve, apparently at one of the yearly feasts—Passover, Weeks, or Booths (cf. Deut 16:1–17), upon whom reproach as been a burden. Yahweh will deal with those who oppress Israel. For the expression "deal with" meaning "meting out judgment," see Ezek 22:14; 23:25, 29. Yahweh will save those walking with a limp and assemble all those banished to foreign lands (Ezek 34:16; Mic 4:6–7). These he will make a praise and a name (Deut 26:19), those who bore shame in exile. Yahweh repeats his promise, saying he will gather exiles among all peoples of the earth and make them a name and a praise, whose shame has been over all the earth! He will bring them home and make them a name and a praise among all peoples of earth (cf. Isa 52:10). This climax to the promise of restoration will happen when Yahweh restores the people's fortunes before their eyes.

With Zephaniah speaking this wonderful word of hope after his searing word of judgment, was he assuming that judgment would indeed take place, and restoration come later—much later? This is what is preached by Jeremiah (Jer 30–33), as well as some of the eighth century prophets (Hosea; Micah, Isaiah). Both Jeremiah and Zephaniah seem to have known the Song of Moses in Deut 32, which in my view was the lawbook found in the temple in 622.[2] There it is shown that in the economy of God history for Israel begins and ends in salvation.

## REFLECTION

1. How important is it to wait for the Lord? Do you find this difficult? Aristotle (384–322) is reported to have said "Patience is bitter, but its fruit is sweet." The Roman statesman Cato the Elder (234–149) said: "Of human virtues, patience is the greatest." In the New Testament, see Paul's words in Rom 8:25.

2. Do you think it possible for the Lord to change vile speech into pure speech, or just secular speech into speech that calls upon the name of the Lord? Can deceitful tongues be entirely done away with?

3. Do rebellious deeds against God or others bring shame, or do some people just get away with them?

4. Have you ever sung loudly or shouted for joy when the Lord brought you deliverance? Zephaniah says the Lord, too, rejoices with joy and loud singing. See what Jesus says about joy in heaven over one sinner who repents (Luke 15:7).

---

2. Lundbom, "Lawbook of the Josianic Reform"; Lundbom, *Jeremiah 1–20*, 106.

# NAHUM

# 7

# "YAHWEH IS TAKING VENGEANCE ON HIS ADVERSARIES" (1:2–11)

1 ²*A jealous and avenging God is Yahweh*
　*Yahweh avenges and is lord of wrath*
*Yahweh avenges against his adversaries*
　*and he maintains it against his enemies*
³*Yahweh is slow to anger but great in power*
　*and will by no means acquit the guilty*
*Yahweh's way is in whirlwind and in storm*
　*and clouds the dust of his feet*
⁴*He rebukes the sea and makes it dry*
　*and all the rivers he dries up*
*Languishing are Bashan and Carmel*
　*and the bud of Lebanon is languishing*
⁵*The mountains quake before him*
　*and the hills melt*
*And the earth is lifted up from before him*
　*yes, the world and all who inhabit it*

>⁶*Before his indignation who can stand?*
>  *and who can arise in the heat of his anger?*
>  *His wrath is poured out like fire*
>    *and by him rocks are broken in pieces*
>⁷*Yahweh is good*
>    *as a stronghold in a day of distress*
>      *and he knows those who seek refuge in him*
>⁸*But in an overflowing flood*
>    *he will make a full end of her place*
>      *and his enemies he will pursue into darkness*
>⁹*What do you plot against Yahweh?*
>    *he will make a full end*
>      *distress will not arise a second time*
>¹⁰*Indeed even like entangled thorns*
>    *and like imbibed drunkards*
>      *they are fully consumed like dry chaff*
>¹¹*From you went forth*
>    *one who plotted evil against Yahweh*
>      *who counseled worthless ideas.*

## RHETORIC AND COMPOSITION

This opening prophecy of Nahum continues to 1:11 where, in the Hebrew Bible, a section occurs. The messenger formula in 1:12 begins a new oracle. Nahum 1:2–9 shows signs of being an original acrostic (Driver; Smith; Roberts), but changes in the text are required to restore it. Like acrostics, however, the poetry has no logical progression. From beginning to end it is concerned with Yahweh's wrath against his foes, just now Assyria and its capital Nineveh.

It is possible that "worthless" in 1:11 is a catchword to "worthless" in 1:15. If so, the oracle in 1:12–14 can be taken as a later addition.

Nahum is an extraordinary poet, his poetry being filled with repetition, inverted syntax, embellishment, and an array of colorful expressions. In the present passage he begins with this repetition and inverted syntax:

> ²A jealous and *avenging* God is *Yahweh*
> *Yahweh avenges* and is lord of wrath
> *Yahweh avenges against* his adversaries
> and he maintains it *against* his enemies.

In 1:1–3 the divine name Yahweh occurs five times. In 1:4 is more inverted syntax:

> ⁴*Languishing* are Bashan and Carmel
> and the bud of Lebanon *is languishing*

Another repetition occurs in 1:6, again with inverted syntax:

> ⁶Before his indignation / *who* can stand?
> and *who* can arise / in the heat of his anger?

In 1:8–9 is this repetition:

> ⁸*he will make a full end* of her place
> . . . . . . . . . . . . . . . .
> *he will make a full end*

In 1:9–11 is an inclusio:

> ⁹⁻¹¹What do you *plot against Yahweh*?
> . . . . . . . .
> one who *plotted* evil *against Yahweh*
> . . . . . . . . . . . .

## MESSAGE

Nahum opens his prophecies and begins the present one by stating that Yahweh is a jealous and avenging God, one who is lord/owner of wrath, one who loathes worship of other gods (cf. Exod 20:5; 34:14; Deut 4:24; 6:15), one who can be counted on to punish wrongdoing, especially among his enemies (cf. Isa 42:13). On the expression "lord/owner" of wrath, see Prov 22:24; 29:22. "Maintaining wrath" or "bearing a grudge" is otherwise denied of God and human beings (Lev 19:18; Jer 3:5; Ps 103:9). Nahum is familiar, as any good prophet would be, with the Decalogue where the covenant people are similarly warned: "For I Yahweh your God am a jealous God, punishing children for the iniquity of their parents, to the third and fourth generation of those who reject me" (Exod 20:5). The word "jealousy" carries largely negative connotations in English, and it may seem inappropriate to apply this word to God. But Roberts says quite correctly: "The statement that Yahweh is a jealous God (*ĕl qannô*) is a statement about God's self-respect; he will not be treated as merely one among many, nor will he allow his demands to be ignored."[1] Heschel, however, betrays an uneasiness over the term, saying that elsewhere and in the present passage the meaning of the term is, "I am a God above jealousy and jealousy is not master of Me."[2]

Nahum is stating Yahweh's readiness to pour out wrath upon one city whose kings, armies, and emissaries have insulted and greatly oppressed the covenant people (2 Kgs 18:13–35; Isa 36:1–20), a city he will later name (Nah 2:8). Yahweh is an avenging God (Deut 32:21; Isa 59:17), especially against enemies (Isa 1:24; Ezek 25:14; Isa 61:2; 63:4). Jeremiah, too, calls for Yahweh's vengeance upon his foes (Jer 11:20; 50:15, 28; 51:6; etc.), and Ezekiel knows that Yahweh has a jealous wrath and is jealous for his holy name (Ezek 36:5–7; 39:25).

Nahum then cites the classic confession of Yahweh's character. Yahweh is a God slow to anger, great in power, but one who will by no means acquit the guilty (1:3; Exod

1. Roberts, *Nahum*, 49.
2. Heschel, *Prophets*, 283n.

34:6–7; Num 14:18; Joel 2:13; Ps 86:15; etc.). Roberts rightly notes that in most confessional statements the emphasis is upon Yahweh's mercy, his slowness to anger, and his willingness to forgive, but here Nahum is putting the emphasis on Yahweh being a God of harsh judgment. The addition of "great in power," found in no other confession of the divine nature, supports this. Turning to the natural order, Nahum says that Yahweh's way is in the whirlwind and the storm (Isa 29:6); clouds are but dust of his feet. Yahweh rebukes the sea and makes it dry, also makes rivers dry up (1:4; Ps 66:6; Isa 44:27; 50:2b). Yahweh is remembered in the exodus as enabling Israel to pass through the Sea on dry land (Pss 77:19 [Heb 77:20]; 106:9; cf. Exod 14:2 9; 15:19b; Isa 51:10). Later on, when Israel was about to cross into Canaan, Yahweh dried up the Jordan (Josh 4:22–23; Ps 74:15). When Yahweh sends a drought the ever-flowing streams (Ar: *wadis*) dry up (1 Kgs 17:7).

Bashan in north Trans-Jordan, Carmel on the Mediterranean, and Lebanon to the north are all noted for their luxurious growth and majestic stands of trees (Isa 2:13; 33:9; 35:2), but these wither and die at the blast of Yahweh's nostrils. A severe drought is implied. Lebanon's buds are those on its famous cedar trees, depicted here as drooping (cf. Joel 1:12). Ps 29:5 says that Yahweh's voice breaks the cedars of Lebanon. Yahweh's nasal blast is seen most dramatically in the sirocco, that strong east wind off the desert, drying up things in an instant (Hos 13:15; Isa 40:7; Jer 4:11–12; 13:24; 18:17). Yes, when Yahweh is angry mountains quake and hills melt, the latter probably meaning that they are overcome by torrents of water (Mic 1:4; Hab 3:10). Nahum has returned to effects of the storm (cf. Ps 18:7; Hab 3:6). The earth erupts in Yahweh's presence, at times seemingly the entire world and all who inhabit it (cf. Jer 4:24–25). When Yahweh is angry earthquakes occur.

Before Yahweh's indignation who can stand? (Amos 7:2; Jer 10:10). Can anyone arise in the heat of Yahweh's anger? The questions are rhetorical, and while applicable to any nation, here they speak to Yahweh's judgment on Nineveh. Yahweh's wrath pours out like fire (Jer 7:20; 44:6). From the Elijah stories we learn that fire symbolizes total destruction (2 Kgs 1:10, 12).[3] Yahweh's stormwind and lightning also break rocks in pieces (1 Kgs 19:11a; Jer 23:29).

But Yahweh is good. Here and in the following verse Nahum addresses a Judahite audience (Driver; Roberts). Yahweh is a stronghold in the day of distress, knowing and caring for those who seek refuge in him (Jer 16:19; Ps 37:39). But the prophet is quick to add that Yahweh can nevertheless be an overflowing flood, and for the first time he hints that the current focus is on Nineveh. When Nahum says Yahweh will make a full end of "her place," he is talking about Nineveh, capital of Assyria (Driver)—a reversal of what occurred during the reigns of Ahaz and Manasseh when both Judahite kings did Assyria's bidding. Isaiah said earlier that Assyria's "mighty flood waters ... would sweep into Judah as a flood" (Isa 8:5–8). Yahweh now is bringing an overflowing flood upon Assyria, and will pursue his enemy into darkness. "Darkness" means no escape and an end for Assyria (cf. Job 18:18). Roberts thinks "darkness" alludes to Sheol, the realm of the dead.

Nahum now addresses his preferred subject, i.e., Nineveh, not Judah (*pace* Roberts). What is Nineveh plotting against Yahweh, against whom it is folly to devise plans (cf. Hos 7:15)? Yahweh will make a full end of the city. With the rise of the Babylonians and other adversaries distress in the city will not happen twice. Nineveh will fall once and for all. Its "thorn-hedged" defenses and love of drunken feasts will, like dry chaff, be consumed in the flames! So it

3. Heschel, *Prophets*, 16.

*Yahweh Is Taking Vengeance on His Adversaries*

will be for this proud city that plotted evil and entertained worthless ideas against Yahweh.

REFLECTION

1. Do you think of God in the Old Testament as one characterized only by anger, vengeance, and punishment, and in the New Testament replaced by a God of love? Think again. On God's love in the Old Testament, see Deut 4:37; 7:7–8; 10:15; Jer 31:3; etc. As for God's punishment, the church fathers said it was greater in the New Testament than the Old because there sinners were condemned to an eternal Gehenna (hell).

2. Do you see the power and might of God in workings of nature—in hurricanes, tornados, earthquakes, drying up of great rivers, and immense fire damage to treasured forests?

3. Do you agree with Nahum that God is good? Give examples shown in your life.

4. Assyria oppressed Israel and Judah for years, bringing down the Northern Kingdom of Israel in 722—and Sennacherib almost ending things for Judah in 701. Does it not make sense that Nahum and his contemporaries in Judah would express great joy in seeing Assyria on the brink of falling to the Babylonians and Medes in 612?

# 8

# "I WILL BREAK ITS YOKE-BAR FROM UPON YOU" (1:12–14)

1 <sup>12</sup>*Thus said Yahweh:*
*Though at full strength and also many*
   *even so they are cut off and he will pass away*
*Yes I have afflicted you*
   *but I will afflict you no more*
<sup>13</sup>*And now I will break his yoke-bar from upon you*
   *and your straps I will burst asunder*
<sup>14</sup>*Yes, Yahweh has commanded concerning you:*
   *no more will your name be sown*
*From the house of your gods I will cut off*
   *the carved image and the moulton image*
*I will make your grave*
   *for you are of small account.*

*I Will Break Its Yoke-bar from Upon You*

## RHETORIC AND COMPOSITION

This prophecy is delimited in the Hebrew Bible by section markings before 1:12 and after 1:14. A messenger formula also begins a new prophecy in 1:12. There has been uncertainty about 1:15, which in the Hebrew Bible is numbered 2:1. It is a word of glad tidings to Judah, and the question is does it go with the prior oracle to Judah or precede the following judgment upon Nineveh? I opt for the latter, which supports the Hebrew numbering of the verse as 2:1. Driver, Roberts and Achtemeier opt for the former.

I suggested earlier that "worthless" appears to be a catchword between 1:11 and 1:15, which would make the present oracle to Judah a later interpolation.

The prophet here is addressing two audiences:

> Judah is addressed with hope (1:12–13)
> Assyria is addressed with judgment (1:14)

Nahum continues with his repetitive language:

> ¹²Yes *I have afflicted you*
>     but *I will afflict you* no more

## MESSAGE

Nahum in this oracle speaks first to people of Judah. Though the Assyrian army is at full strength and is many in number, it will be sheared as sheep and its king will pass away. Yes, Yahweh has afflicted his people, but he will afflict them no more. He will break the yoke-bar of the Assyrian king and its straps he will cast asunder. Isaiah made this promise to Judah earlier (Isa 10:24–27; 14:25b). Jeremiah prophesied the same later about Babylon (Jer 30:8), but would he have agreed with Nahum that Yahweh in 612 would afflict Judah no longer?

In 1:14 Nahum turns to address Assyria. Yahweh has a command concerning this once mighty nation: No more will its name be perpetuated; carved and molten images in houses (temples) of its gods—Assur, Ishtar, Anu, Shamash, and others—which Ahaz imported into the Jerusalem temple (2 Chr 28:2), and which were again imported into Judah during the reign of Manasseh (2 Kgs 21:1–15), will be cut off. Yahweh will make Nineveh's grave; the city is of small account.

## REFLECTION

1. Nahum's judgment against Nineveh was fulfilled. What about his prophecy of hope for Judah? Was that fulfilled, and if so, when?

2. God's covenant with Israel was likened to a yoking with straps. Jeremiah said Judah had broken the yoke-bar and straps (Jer 2:20; 5:5). When Jesus tells his followers: "Take my yoke upon you, and learn from me; for I am gentle and humble in heart, and you will find rest for your souls" (Matt 11:29 NRSV), might he be talking about the new covenant?

3. Recall what the Decalogue says about Israel making and worshiping idols (Exod 20:4–6; Deut 5:8–10). What idols do we worship today?

4. Why do you think Jeremiah is silent about Nineveh's fall in 612? Should he not have celebrated the moment? Perhaps he left the prophecy to Nahum, or might there have been another reason for Jeremiah's silence about Nineveh?

# 9

# "LOOK UPON THE MOUNTAINS: ONE WHO BRINGS GOOD TIDINGS!" (1:15—2:13 [HEB 2:1-14])

1 *15Look upon the mountains the feet of him*
   *who brings good tidings*
      *who bears news of peace!*
*Keep your pilgrimage feasts, O Judah*
   *pay your vows*
*For never again will the worthless pass through you*
   *it is utterly cut off*
2 *1A scatterer has come up against you*
   *guard the siege-works*
      *watch the road*
*Make strong your loins*
   *strengthen your power mightily*
*2For Yahweh is bringing back the pride of Jacob*
   *like the pride of Israel*

## NAHUM

*For plunderers have plundered them*
  *and their branches they have ruined*
³*The shield of his mighty men is red*
  *soldiers are clad in scarlet*
*The iron of the chariots flash*
  *in the day of his preparation*
    *and the spears are made to shake*
⁴*The chariots go madly in the streets*
  *they rush to and fro through the squares*
*Their appearance like torches*
  *they dart like lightning*
⁵*He remembers his majestic ones*
  *they stumble in their march*
*They hasten to her wall*
  *and the mantelet[1] is prepared*
⁶*The river gates are opened*
  *and the palace melts away*
⁷*Yes it is fixed, she is stripped, she is carried off*
  *her handmaids moaning*
*Like the sound of doves*
  *beating upon their breasts*
⁸ *Yes, Nineveh has been like a pool of water for days*
  *and they run away*
    *"stop! stop!" but none makes a turn*
⁹*Take spoil of silver*
  *take spoil of gold!*
*There is no end to the supply*
  *an abundance of every precious thing*
¹⁰*Desolate and desolation and ruin!*
  *yes heart is faint and knees tremble*
*Anguish is on all loins*
  *all their faces grow pale!*
¹¹*Where is the den of the lions*
  *and the pasture for the young lions*
*Where lion, lioness, and lion's cubs walked*
  *and none disturbed?*

---

1. A moveable shelter for those working to breach the city wall.

*Look Upon the Mountains: One Who Brings Good Tidings!*

> ¹²*The lion tore enough for its cubs*
> *and strangled for his lionesses*
> *It filled its caves with prey*
> *and its dens with torn flesh*
> ¹³*Look, I am against you, oracle of Yahweh of hosts*
> *and I will burn her chariots in smoke*
> *and your young lions the sword will devour*
> *I will cut off your prey from the earth*
> *and the voice of your messengers will no longer bear news.*

## RHETORIC AND COMPOSITION

These verses are 2:1–15 in the Hebrew Bible, where they are delimited by sections before 2:1 [Eng 1:15] and after 2:14 [Eng 2:13]. The final verse containing an oracle formula, which the RSV and NRSV print as prose, can easily be scanned as poetry (so *BHQ*).

The passage was linked earlier to 1:1–11 by the catchword "worthless" in 1:11 and 15. Now it is linked to the preceding by the catchword "cut off" in 1:14 and 1:15. To the following passage it is linked with the catchword "prey" in 2:13 and 3:1.

At beginning and end are the demonstrative particles "Look" (inclusio):

> 1 ¹⁵*Look* on the mountains . . .
> 2 ¹³*Look* I am against you . . .

This repetition and the catchword to 1:14 point to 1:15 belonging to the present oracle, not concluding the preceding oracle (*pace* Driver; Roberts and Achtemeier), also to 2:13 being part of the present prophecy, not an add-on.

For structures using this same particle, see Jer 3:1–5 and 7:8–11.[2]

Two other inclusios support our division and explain why 1:15 is numbered 2:1 in the Hebrew Bible. One inclusio ties together the present unit by repeating forms of the Hebrew verbs *šmʿ* ("hear, proclaim, bear news") and *krt* ("cut off"):

> 1 ¹⁵Look upon the mountains the feet of him
>   who brings good tidings
>     *who bears news* of peace!
> . . . . . . . . . . . . . . . . .
>   *it is utterly cut off*
>
> 2 ¹³ᵇI will *cut off* your prey from the earth
>   and the voice of your messengers *will bear news* no longer.

The second ties the opening verse of the present passage in with the concluding verse of the final woe oracle, once again repeating the verb *šmʿ* ("who bears news / who hear news"):

> 1¹⁵Look upon the mountains the feet of him
>   who brings good tidings
>     *who bears news* of peace!
>
> 3 ¹⁹All *who hear news of you*
>   clap their hands over you
> For upon whom has not passed
>   your continual evil?

In the opening verse Judah hears good news of peace with the fall of Nineveh; in Nahum's final word all who hear the news of Assyria's demise clap their hands in derision over her!

---

2. Lundbom, *Jeremiah 1–20*, 298–99, 453, 457.

The present passage also contains repetition called *geminatio*, which serves to intensify (GKC §123e). These are frequent in prophetic discourse:[3]

> ⁸*"stop! stop!"*. . . . . . . . . .
> ¹⁰*Desolate! Desolation!* . . . . . . . .

The first three words of v. 10 are a wordplay in the Hebrew:

> ¹⁰*Desolate and desolation and ruin!*

Nahum is also seen to make use of rhetorical questions in 2:11.

The present oracle contains a considerable amount of "back and forth" between 1) addresses: Judah; the Assyrian king; Assyria; Nineveh; the attacking enemy; and 2) subjects: good news for Judah; bad news for Assyria; feeble response of the Assyrian defenders; enemy in attack; Nineveh being flooded; Nineveh's citizens fleeing left and right, not heeding the commands to stop; Nineveh's royalty humiliated and taken captive; all Nineveh being faint, trembling, with faces pale white; former prowess of Assyria gone; Nineveh's prey forever cut off; other nations jubilant.

## MESSAGE

We have here the heart of Nahum's message: a graphic oracle about Nineveh being attacked sacked, and wiped off the canvas of history. The prophet begins, however, by addressing his Judahite audience, telling them to "look!" Coming over the mountains is a messenger bringing tidings of peace. How beautiful it is! Similar words are spoken by the unnamed prophet of the exile (Isa 52:7). With peace Judah can now resume her pilgrimage feasts—Passover, Weeks,

3. Lundbom, *Hebrew Prophets*, 168.

and Booths (Deut 16:1–17). Once again people can come to the temple to pay their vows (Deut 23:21–23), which are now due. Worthless Assyria, which so many times has passed through Northern Israel and Judah, making life miserable for the covenant people, will do so no longer, for it is entirely cut off.

Background for this prophecy is the combined attack of Babylon and the Medes on Nineveh in 612. After a three-month siege the city was taken and destroyed. The Bible otherwise says nothing about this momentous event, commenting only on a later battle in 609 between Egypt, an Assyrian remnant, and Babylon, when Josiah while trying to stop Neco was slain by the Pharaoh at Megiddo (2 Kgs 24:29–30; 2 Chr 35:20–24). It also reports the battle in 605 between Egypt and Babylon at Carchemish, where Nebuchadnezzar and his army sent Egypt reeling in defeat (Jer 46:2). All these events are documented in the Babylonian Chronicle (BM 21946; obv. 1–7; cf. *ANET*[3] 303–5) and in Josephus.[4]

Nahum turns to address the Assyrian king, telling him what he probably already knows, that a "scatterer" (an enemy) has come up against him. The "scatterer" is not Yahweh (*pace* Roberts). In the next verse Yahweh is said to be acting through the "scatterer" to restore the pride of Jacob/Israel. The king is ironically told to guard the siege-works and watch the road. It will have little effect! Jeremiah similarly gives hopeless commands to Egyptian fighters when Egypt is on the Euphrates making a last-ditch attempt to save Assyria (Jer 46:3–6). The Assyrian king should also see to it that all warriors make strong their loins wherein their strength lies (cf. Amos 2:14), i.e., that all warriors exercise courage. Then, almost parenthetically, Nahum says that in this battle Yahweh is restoring the (good) pride of

4. Josephus, *Ant.* 10.84–86.

*Look Upon the Mountains: One Who Brings Good Tidings!*

Jacob/Israel (cf. Ps 47:4), where Jacob/Israel here refers to Judah (Driver). In citing the former pride of Jacob/Israel Nahum may have in mind a united Israel under David and Solomon. Plunderers of the brutal Assyrian nation emptied Judah's cities (Nah 3:1; cf. Jer 51:2), rendering them ruined branches of once luxuriant vines.

The next two verses describe the attack on Nineveh by a coalition of Babylon and the Medes. Shields of the attacking commander's fighters are blood red, his solders smartly clad in scarlet. In preparation for battle iron on the chariots flash (Joel 2:5) and spears shake wildly. The attack begins, and chariots are seen rushing madly in Nineveh's (suburban) streets and squares (cf. Jer 46:9). Like torches at night they dart back and forth like lightning.

The Assyrian king (so Driver) remembers his commanders; they are summoned, but stumble as they march. The enemy hastens to the city wall and sets up a protective canopy for the siege (cf. Joel 2:7). River gates are opened and the palace is dissolved in a flood of water (cf. 1:5a). Attackers pour into the city. What follows is predetermined: The fleeing queen, queen mother, or another woman of royalty is seized, stripped of her clothes, and carried off. Her maidens moan like doves, beating their breasts.

With the river gates opened Nineveh has been a pool of water for days, and its people are fleeing. They are told to stop, but no one does. The sack of the city is described. Attackers cry, "Take silver, take gold as spoil." Nineveh has a great supply of both. "Put your hands on every precious thing!" The scene is one of desolation and ruin; hearts melt in fear and knees tremble uncontrollably. Anguish is on all loins (cf. Ps 69:23); all faces are pale white (cf. Jer 30:6; Joel 2:6).

The prophet proceeds to taunt Assyria with rhetorical questions. Where now is the lions' den, the feeding ground of young lions? Nineveh was a notorious lion in the ancient world—cruel and merciless with nations they had conquered. Is the place where lions, lionesses, and cubs walked unopposed completely gone? In prior days the lion of Assyria tore enough flesh for its cubs and strangled more for its mate. Its lairs in the ground were filled with prey (3:1), the torn flesh of many it had conquered. Assyria had been a ruthless nation.[5]

Nahum concludes with an oracle from Yahweh of hosts: Yahweh is against Nineveh; he will burn its chariots with fire, and the sword will devour its young lions, which could be Egypt or others defending Assyria. Yahweh will cut off all the prey Assyria has consumed over the years, and the voice of its messengers bringing bad news to Judah and other nations will be heard no more. Nahum here makes a stark contrast to messengers bringing good news at the beginning of the oracle.

REFLECTION

1. In the New Testament it is apostles (messengers) who bear the gospel (good news). Who are the messengers of good news today?

2. Might Nahum have been a bit overly optimistic in saying that with the defeat of Assyria Yahweh was now restoring the pride of Jacob/Israel? What might Jeremiah have been saying in his corner of the temple courtyard?

3. Are there nations today who behave like lions in search of prey? Name some.

4. Who were Assyria's messengers no longer to be heard (cf. 2 Kgs 16:7; 18:17; 19:4, 9, 14, 23)?

5. Heschel, *Prophets*, 162–63.

10

# "WOE TO THE BLOODY CITY!" (3:1-19)

3 ¹*Woe to the bloody city*
   *all of it full of lying and booty*
      *no end to the prey!*
²*The sound of the whip, and sound of rattling wheels*
   *galloping horses and leaping chariots!*
³*Horsemen mounting*
   *and flashing sword and glittering spear*
*And hosts of the slain*
   *and an abundance of corpses*
*Yes, no end of dead bodies*
   *they stumble over their bodies!*
⁴*Because of the many harlotries of the harlot*
   *well-charming mistress of sorceries*
*Who sells nations with her harlotries*
   *and families with her sorceries*

⁵*Look I am against you, oracle of Yahweh of hosts*
   *and I will lift up your skirts over your face*

*And I will let nations see your nakedness*
　*and kingdoms your shame*
*⁶I will throw filth upon you and treat you with contempt*
　*and I will make you a spectacle*
*⁷Then all who see you will flee from you*
　*and say, "Devastated is Nineveh, who will wildly lament her?"*
　　*from where will I seek comforters for you?*

*⁸Are you better than No-Amon[1]*
　*that sat by the Nile-canals*
　　*waters surrounding her*
*Whose rampart[2] was the sea*
　　*water her walls?[3]*
*⁹Cush[4] and Egypt were her might*
　*and there was no end*
*Put and the Libyans[5]*
　*they were her[6] helpers*
*¹⁰Even she became exiles*
　*she went into captivity*
*Even her little ones were dashed in pieces*
　*at the head of all the streets*
*And upon her honored ones lots were cast*
　*and all her great ones were bound in chains*
*¹¹Even you will become drunk*
　*you will become unconscious*
*Even you will seek*
　*a dwelling place from the enemy*
*¹²All your fortresses are fig trees with first-ripe figs*

1. Amon was the local god of No (Gk: Thebes), capital of Upper Egypt.

2. A small surrounding outer wall.

3. Adopting with Roberts the reading of 4QpNah; MT has "her walls from the sea"; Tg. has "the waters of the sea her wall."

4. Ethiopia.

5. Put and Libyans were North African peoples (cf. Gen 10:6).

6. Reading "her" with the LXX; MT has "your."

> *if shaken they fall into the mouth of the eater*
> [13] *Look your people are women in your midst*
>    *the gates of your land are wide open to your enemies*
>       *fire has devoured your bars*
> [14] *Draw for yourselves water for the siege*
>    *strengthen your forts*
> *Go into the clay*
>    *and tread the mortar*
>       *take hold of the brickmold!*
> [15] *There fire will consume you*
>    *a sword will cut you off*
>       *it will consume you like the young locust*
> *Multiply like the young locust*
>    *multiply like the swarming locust!*
> [16] *You increased your traders*
>    *more than the stars of the heavens*
>       *the young locust strips itself and flies away*
> [17] *Your princes are like swarming locusts*
>    *your scribes like swarms of locusts*
>       *which settle on the stone walls on a cold day*
> *When the sun rises they flee*
>    *it is not known to what place they go*
> [18] *Your shepherds are asleep O king of Assyria*
>    *your majestic ones are at rest*
> *Your people are scattered on the mountains*
>    *with none to gather them*
> [19] *No one is alleviating your wound*
>    *your blow is grievous*
> *All who hear news of you*
>    *clap their hands over you*
> *For upon whom has not passed*
>    *your continual evil?*

## RHETORIC AND COMPOSITION

The present verses are delimited in the Hebrew Bible by a section before 3:1, which is also the chapter division. Verse

19 of chapter 3 is the end of the book. An oracle formula in 3:5 introduces a word from Yahweh midpoint in the prophecy (3:5–7). The passage is linked to the previous one by the catchword "prey" in 2:13 and 3:1.

Nahum uses an expression found also in Jeremiah:

| Nah 3:5 | *I will lift up your skirts over your face* | Jer 13:26 | *I myself will lift up your skirts over your face* |

The passage has an abundance of repeated vocabulary. In 3:10–11 is a fourfold repetition of *gam* ("even"), which is *anaphora*:

> ¹⁰*Even* she (Thebes) became exiles
> . . . . . . . . . . . . . . .
> *Even* (Thebes's) little ones were dashed in pieces
> . . . . . . . . . . . . . . .
> ¹¹*Even* you (Nineveh) also will become drunk
> . . . . . . . . . . . . . . .
> *Even* you (Nineveh) will seek
> . . . . . . . . . . . . . . .

In addition to the repetitions is a change of subject/addressee at the center.

The passage has an alternation of speaking voices:

| 3:1–4 | Nahum speaks |
| 3:5–7 | Yahweh speaks |
| 3:8–19 | Nahum speaks |

Nahum employs rhetorical questions in 3:7b–8, and in 3:17 "swarms of locusts" is a wordplay (paronomasia) in the Hebrew.

## MESSAGE

In this final passage Nahum continues his condemnation of Nineveh, a city filled with bloodshed, lying, and booty taken from other nations. The lying could be false promises to weaker nations of help or protection to get them into its power (Driver). "Prey" like "booty" is a term suggesting torn flesh eaten by hungry lions (cf. 2:11–12). Nahum's "woe" on the city is strong, just short of a curse, pronounced often by prophets on cities or evildoers wherever they reside. On the term, see Message for "But Yahweh Is in His Holy Temple" (Hab 2:6b–20) with references.

In 3:2–3 the attack and sack of Nineveh is again described in vivid detail. Horses are galloping (cf. Judg 5:22), and one can hear the crack of the whip. Wheels of bouncing chariots are rattling (cf. 2:4; Jer 46:9a; Joel 2:5; Rev 9:9). Horsemen mount with glittering swords in hand. Devastation of human life is everywhere. Dead bodies lie in heaps, so many there are that survivors are stumbling over them. Destruction is because of the countless harlotries of Nineveh the harlot (cf. Prov 6:26; 7:10–23). She has been a charming mistress of sorcery, an abominable secret art used to lure nations into subjection and an import into other nations, one of which was Judah (cf. Mic 5:12 [Heb 5:11]; Jer 27:9; Isa 47:9b).

In 3:5–7 Yahweh intervenes as speaker. He is against this wicked city (cf. 2:13), and will lift up her skirts over her face; all nations can then gaze upon her shame while she herself is unable to view the humiliation (cf. Jer 13:22, 26; Lam 1:8–9; Hos 2:3a, 10 [Heb 2:5a, 12]; Ezek 16:36–39). Yahweh will treat harlot Nineveh with contempt, throwing filth on her and making her a spectacle (cf. Lam 1:17). All who see the ruined city will flee in horror. Who will lament this once great city now lying in rubble? Apparently a standard question (Jer 15:5; Isa 51:19). No one. In 3:19b those hearing news of her fall will clap their hands. Yahweh concludes with another rhetorical question: From where can he seek comforters for Nineveh? There are none. Jerusalem later discovered that she, too, had no one to comfort her in her time of need (Jer 15:5; Lam 1:2, 9, 16–17, 21; Isa 51:19).

Nahum returns as speaker in 3:8 to complete the prophecy. Is Nineveh and its gods any better than Thebes and its god Amon Rē, that sat by canals of the Nile with waters surrounding her? Thebes was the capital of Upper Egypt from the time of the Middle Kingdom (ca. 2000). For an ancient hymn written to Amen Râ (= Amon Rē), see *ANET*[3] 365–67. The "sea" here refers to the Nile (cf. Isa 19:5), but Thebes' location nevertheless appears to be idealized (Driver; Smith). While the city lay east of the Nile, even with the known risings of this great river, it could hardly be portrayed as bounded or protected by its canals.

Ethiopia and all Egypt were the might of Thebes. Nahum again uses the expression "and there was no end" (see 2:9 [Heb 2:10] and 3:3). It occurred earlier in Isa 2:7 (2x). Put and Libyan, peoples of North Africa, were also her helpers. But where is Thebes now? Assurbanipal destroyed Thebes ca. 663. The Assyrian king claims he took booty beyond counting—including two obelisks standing at the door of the temple—and brought it all to Assyria (*ANET*[3] 295). Jeremiah and Ezekiel pronounced a later judgment upon Thebes (Jer 46:24–26; Ezek 30:14–16). Survivors of this great city were carried into captivity, just as Tiglath-pileser did with survivors from Galilee and Transjordan in 733 (2 Kgs 15:29), Sargon II with survivors from Samaria in 722 (2 Kgs 17:6; 18:11), and Sennacherib with survivors from forty-six Judahite cities in 701 (*ANET*[3] 288; cf. 2 Kgs 18:13; Isa 1:4–9). The same happened to countless other nations. For pictures of Sennacherib's campaigns, see *ANEP*[2] 371–74. Jerusalem later discovered in her day of collapse that no helpers could be found (Lam 1:7). Thebes's little ones lay dashed in pieces at the head of every street (cf. 2 Kgs 8:12; Isa 13:16; 51:20; Hos 10:14b). Was the enemy happy about such cruelty? (cf. Ps 137:9). As I write, in November of 2023, a war between Israel and Hamas rages, and concern is widespread for babies lying helpless in Gaza's al-Shifa hospital (cf. Lam 2:11–12, 19). A further indignity for Thebes was that lots were cast for its surviving nobles (cf. Joel 3:3 [Heb 4:3]), and leading citizens were put in chains and carried away to who knows where? (cf. Jer 39:7; 40:1).

Now the unthinkable has occurred. Nahum says the cup of wrath has been passed to you, Nineveh. You will drink and become drunk; you will stagger and become unconscious (cf. Jer 25:15–29; Lam 4:21; Ps 60:3 [Heb 60:5]; Isa 52:17–18); you will seek refuge in some dwelling of the enemy but probably will not find one. All your celebrated fortresses have become like first-ripe figs: if shaken from the tree they fall into the mouth of the eater.

Those remaining in Nineveh are told to look around: people have become women in their midst (Isa 19:16; Jer 50:37; 51:30). One of the standard curses of antiquity was that a defeated or near-defeated people—soldiers in particular—had become like (weak) women. Jeremiah portrayed the distressed man/soldier, bereft of courage, like a woman in labor (Jer 30:6; 49:22). In an ancient Hittite text titled "A Soldier's Oath" (*ANET*[3] 354), defeated soldiers could look forward to the indignity of being clothed in women's dress and made to carry a distaff[7] and mirror in hand. Will the captured defenders of Nineveh be paraded in the streets, dressed as women carrying a distaff and vanity mirror? Gates of fortifications around Nineveh are now wide open to the enemy; bars securing them are consumed by fire. With the outer defenses open, Ninevites are told to prepare for a siege of the city. Nahum resorts to bitter irony. "Draw for yourselves water for the siege; strengthen your forts. Go

---

7. A rod on which wool or flax is wound in preparation for spinning, held up here as a symbol of women's work.

into the clay and tread the mortar; take hold of the brickmold!" Sun-dried bricks will be needed to repair breeches in the wall. It will be to no avail. Destruction awaits the city. Fire will consume it, the sword will cut it down, and it will be devoured as trees and vegetation are devoured by young locusts (Joel 1:4). Multiply yourself for the slaughter! the prophet says.

Nineveh was a great commercial center, its traders being without number. But its busy merchant population will be like the young locust shedding its skin and flying away. Nineveh's princes and scribes—the latter doubtless being many during the literary reign of Assurbanipal (Smith)—are now but swarms of locusts on a stone wall on a cold day (Joel 2:7, 9). When the sun rises they fly away, and no one knows where they have gone. It is well known that when locusts leave they do so quickly and fly to unknown destinations.

The prophecy has a closing word for the king of Assyria. His shepherds (officials and nobles) are sleeping a perpetual sleep; they lie scattered on the mountains with none to gather them (cf. 1 Kgs 22:17; Jer 9:22 [Heb 9:21]). There is no one alleviating your wound, says the prophet; the blow you have received is grievous (cf. Jer 30:12–13; 46:11). All who hear news of your demise will hiss and clap their hands in derision (cf. Jer 19:8; 49:17; 50:13; Lam 2:15; Ezek 25:6). For upon whom have your continual evil deeds not been visited?

## REFLECTION

1. What sort of harlotries and sorceries might people be engaged in today?

2. Nahum imagines Nineveh's people being taken into captivity, and its small children dashed in pieces in

the streets. War is cruel, but is it as cruel today as it was then?

3. Do you ever think leaders of our country are unaware of the devastation going on?
4. Can you recall in some time of grief how important it was to have someone comfort you?

# HABAKKUK

# 11

# "A WORK IS BEING DONE IN YOUR DAYS" (1:2-17)

> 1 ²*How long, O Yahweh, will I cry for help*
>    *and you will not hear?*
> *I cry out to you "Violence!"*
>    *and you will not save?*
> ³*Why do you make me see iniquity*
>    *and look upon mischief?*
> *And devastation and violence before me*
>    *and there is contention and strife rising up?*
> ⁴*Therefore the law is ineffective*
>    *and justice never goes forth*
> *For the wicked surround the righteous*
>    *therefore justice goes forth crooked*
> ⁵*Look among the nations and take notice*
>    *and be astounded and astound yourselves!*
> *For I am working a work in your days*
>    *that you would not believe if it were told*
> ⁶*For look, I am raising up the Chaldeans*
>    *that fierce and impetuous nation*

*That marches through the wide expanses of the earth*
  *to possess dwellings not its own*
⁷*Terrible and dreadful is it*
  *its justice and dignity proceeds from itself*
⁸*And its horses are swifter than leopards*
  *and keener than evening wolves*
    *and its horsemen charge about*
*Yes, its horsemen come from afar*
  *they fly like an eagle swift to devour*
⁹*Each one of them comes for violence*
  *their faces all set forward*
    *and he gathers captives like sand*
¹⁰*Yes he mocks with kings*
  *and rulers he derides*
*He laughs at every fortress*
  *and he heaps up dirt and takes it*
¹¹*Then the wind sweeps on*
  *but he transgresses and becomes guilty*
    *this his strength becomes his god!*

¹²*Are you not from of old*
  *O Yahweh my God, my Holy One?*
    *we will not die!*[1]
*O Yahweh, for justice you have ordained him*
  *and O Rock, for correction you have established him*
¹³*Purer eyes than to behold evil*
  *not able to look upon mischief*
*Why then do you look upon the treacherous*
  *you are silent when the wicked swallows*
    *one more righteous than he?*
¹⁴*Yes, you make humans like the fish of the sea*

---

1. The MT reading is one of 18 *tiqqûnê sōpherim* ("corrections of the scribes") in the Hebrew Bible, where an original reading is thought to have been "you will not die," a reading too offensive to God to let stand (Ginsburg, *Introduction,* 348–63; Roberts). Driver, however, thinks this is "probably nothing more than a Jewish fancy," the present reading being better in giving point to the verse. The LXX reading supports MT.

> like creeping things that have no ruler over them
> ¹⁵Every one he brings up with a hook
> he drags him out with his net
> He gathers him in his seine²
> therefore he rejoices and exults
> ¹⁶Therefore he sacrifices to his net
> and burns incense to his seine
> For by them his portion is fat
> and his food plenteous
> ¹⁷Is he therefore to keep emptying his net³
> and continuously slay nations
> and not have compassion?

## RHETORIC AND COMPOSITION

The superscription to this book is minimal: "The burden which the prophet Habakkuk saw." Hebrew "burden" can also mean "oracle" (RSV; NRSV), but Jeremiah disparaged the term, calling it a tired expression used by prophets who report revelations of their own making and not from God (Jer 23:33–40).

The first prophecy begins in 1:2 and ends with a section in the Hebrew Bible after v. 17, which is also the end of the chapter. It is a three-part dialogue between the prophet and Yahweh:

> Habakkuk addresses Yahweh (1:2–4)
> Yahweh answers Habakkuk (1:5–11)
> Habakkuk addresses Yahweh (1:12–17)

In the passage are a number of striking repetitions:

---

2. A fishing net that hangs vertically in the water.
3. 1QpHab has *ḥarbô* his sword") that could give the reading "drawing his sword" (preferred by Roberts).

## HABAKKUK

⁵ *and be astounded, and astound yourselves!*
  For *I am working a work* . . . . . . .

¹⁰*Yes he* mocks with kings
. . . . . . . . . . . . . . . . . . . . .
*and he* heaps up dirt and takes it

¹⁵he drags him out with *his net*
He gathers him in *his seine*

¹⁵*therefore* he rejoices and exults
¹⁶*Therefore* he sacrifices to *his net*
  and burns incense to *his seine*
. . . . . . . . . . . . . . . . . . . . . . . .
¹⁷Is he *therefore* to keep emptying *his net*

## MESSAGE

Habakkuk begins here by asking Yahweh how long he must cry for help and Yahweh not hear (cf. Jer 12:1–2)? He has been crying out "violence" (cf. Jer 20:8), yet Yahweh does not act to save the righteous (cf. Job 19:7). The prophet asks "why" (Pss 10:1; 22:1 [Heb 22:2]; 74:1; Jer 15:18; etc.) he must be made to see naughtiness, mischief to others (Ps 10:7), havoc and violence, contention and strife? They are everywhere! The law by which Judahites are supposed to live is paralyzed; justice in city gates is not being carried out (Jer 5:1, 28). The wicked outnumber the righteous so justice is perverted. Prophets, priests and judges are not doing their jobs (Zeph 3:3–4; Jer 5:31; 6:13–15; 8:7c).

Yahweh answers. He has heard the prophet's cry (cf. Ps 18:6), and matters will be taken care of straightaway. Yahweh tells Habakkuk to look among the nations, for he is doing a work the prophet and all Judah will scarcely believe. The surprise will not be welcomed, rather one they could well do without (Roberts). Yahweh is raising up the Chaldeans from southern Babylonia (Jer 4:5–8), a fierce and impetuous nation that marches through the earth seizing dwellings not their own. Reference may be to the more recent destruction of Nineveh in 612, the follow-up defeat of Assyrians in 609, or the defeat of Egypt and the Assyrian remnant at Carchemish in 605. Nebuchadnezzar may not yet have arrived in the Philistine Plain (Roberts) when he destroyed Ashkelon in 604 and the next year laid waste to Ekron.

Babylon is a terrible nation; its justice and dignity proceeding only from itself. It does whatever it pleases. Its horses run faster than leopards and are keener than evening wolves (Jer 4:13; 5:6; Zeph 3:3). Its horsemen from far away (Jer 5:15) charge about and are swift in seeking someone to devour (Jer 6:22–23). If you think there is violence where you live, O prophet, you have seen nothing; this enemy is known for violence and captures victims like sand. The Babylonian mocks kings and derides rulers; he laughs at every fortress; he heaps up dirt for siege ramps and takes cities. The mighty wind sweeps on, but it will overstep its bounds and become guilty. Its strength is its god.

The prophet answers Yahweh. He knows Yahweh, the Holy One of Israel (Isa 1:4; 5:19, 24; etc.), who is from of timeless antiquity. There must be hope; we will not perish. Yahweh, who is Israel's Rock (Ps 18:2 [Heb 18:3], 31 [Heb 32], 46 [Heb 47]; 19:14 [Heb 19:15]; 28:1; Deut 32:4, 15, 18, 30; etc.), is bringing this foe for justice and correction (cf. Jer 30:11), a "justice" decidedly different from the "justice" in 1:4, and perhaps better translated here as "judgment" (RSV; NRSV). Achtemeier points out that this is a case of *lex talionis*, where Babylonian "justice and violence" will repay Judah for the "violence and crooked justice" it has been practicing in Jerusalem and elsewhere. Yahweh has pure eyes and will not look upon mischief among his people.

Yes, the Babylonians are treacherous, but why does Yahweh remain silent when the wicked swallow up the righteous? Here we have a return of sorts to Habakkuk's prior question in 1:2–4 (Achtemeier), and a striking parallel to the question Jeremiah poses in one of his confessions (Jer 12:1). Yahweh is making humans like fish brought up with hooks or taken into nets (cf. Amos 4:2; Eccl 9:12; Jer 16:16). People are like ants or locusts that have no ruler (Prov 6:6–7; 30:27). The one now gathering them rejoices and gives credit to his net. With the catch his portion is rich and his food plenteous. The prophet closes by asking if this foe is to keep on emptying his net and slaying nations, and not have compassion?

## REFLECTION

1. Do you ever cry to the Lord about wrongdoing and think that he seems not to answer?
2. What can we do today about preachers, judges, and other officials known to be engaged in wrongdoing?
3. How do you feel about a proud, godless nation being used by God to punish his own? Isaiah had to preach this message; so did Jeremiah and Habakkuk.
4. Do you think Habakkuk was satisfied with God's answer to his cry?

## 12

# "THE RIGHTEOUS WILL LIVE BY HIS FAITHFULNESS" (2:1–5)

2 ¹*Upon my watchpost I will stand*
  *and station myself on a tower*
*That I might watch to see what he will say to me*
  *and what I will answer¹ concerning my reproof.*
²*Then Yahweh answered me and said:*
*Write the vision*
  *and make it plain upon the tablets*
    *so he who runs may read it*
³*For the vision is still for an appointed time*
  *it hastens to the end and will not lie*
*If it lingers, wait for it*
  *for it will surely come, it will not delay*
⁴*Look, the puffed up one*
  *his soul is not upright in him*

---

1. Tg has "what I shall be answered"; Driver, Smith, Roberts, and NRSV follow the Syriac Peshitta in reading "what he will answer," or the like. RSV has "what I will answer."

## HABAKKUK

> but the righteous will live by his faithfulness[2]
> [5]Moreover, because wine is treacherous[3]
> the haughty warrior will not rest
> Because his soul is as wide as Sheol[4]
> and like death he is never satisfied
> Yes, he gathers to himself all the nations
> and collects to himself all the peoples.

### RHETORIC AND COMPOSITION

The Hebrew Bible has no sections for this passage, but its beginning is a chapter division, and 2:6a introduces the litany of woes.

Here is another dialogue:

2:1   The prophet speaks a soliloquy
2:2–5   Yahweh answers the prophet's complaint(s)

### MESSAGE

Habakkuk in his complaint asked Yahweh how long this fierce and impetuous foe would go on destroying nations (1:17). Indefinitely? What will happen to Judah? Awaiting a response, the prophet first speaks a soliloquy (Driver). Habakkuk says he will ascend the tower at the corner of the city wall and like a watchman on lookout (cf. 2 Sam 18:24–27; 2 Kgs 9:17) await an answer from Yahweh, after

---

2. Luther translated the Hebrew as *seines Glaubens* (cf. Rom 1:17; 5:1; Gal 3:11; Heb 10:37–39), and was followed by the KJV: "by his faith." The LXX provides no help with ἐκ πίστεώς μου. ("from my faith"). Better is NJPS: "for his fidelity" or NJB: "through faithfulness." Roberts has "its faithfulness."

3. The reading of MT is difficult; Roberts following 1QpHab reads, "How much more shall wealth deceive the arrogant man."

4. The Underworld or place of the dead.

which he will respond regarding his reproof of 1:13–17 (Driver). "Reproof" is strong language, legal and irreverent when speaking to God, yet similar to what comes out of the mouth of Jeremiah in Jer 12:1–2. Prophets typically understood themselves to be "watchmen" (Hos 9:8; Isa 21:6–9; Jer 6:17; Ezek 3:17–21; 33:7), sometimes being faulted for not doing their job (Mic 7:4; Isa 56:10). Habakkuk is concerned about imminent calamity for Judah (cf. 3:16b). Driver says the climb was a "spiritual preparation of the prophet's soul." It may also have been symbolic (Achtemeier), much like the symbolic acts Jeremiah performed (Jer 13:1–11; 19:1–13; 27–28; 32:6–15; 35:1–11; 43:8–13). Habakkuk, like Micah and Jeremiah, must await a word from Yahweh (Mic 7:7; Jer 42:7; cf. Ps 5:3 [Heb 5:4]).

Yahweh comes with an answer. Habakkuk is to write the vision (Nah 1:1) he receives on tablets (Isa 8:1), making the words plain so anyone running past can read them. The vision is also to be written so it can be confirmed at a later time (Driver; Roberts; cf. Isa 30:8). Ward thinks the writing would be on clay tablets of the Babylonian type, but he assumes that the prophecy was written in Babylon, which it was not. More likely the writing was on stones overlaid with plaster, such as Moses was instructed to erect on Mount Ebal once Israel had entered into Canaan (Deut 27:2–8). Tablets may also have been made of wood (Roberts). Assyrian writing boards have turned up in excavations at Nimrud.[5] The vision must await the time Yahweh chooses to fulfill it; the time hastens (lit. "pants") to its end, and it will not disappoint. If it seems to linger, Habakkuk must wait, for it will surely come (cf. Lam 3:25–26)!

What is the content of the vision? Roberts thinks the vision comes in 3:3–15, which assumes the psalm of chapter 3 to be an integral part of Habakkuk's prophecy, which

5. Wiseman, "Assyrian Writing-Boards."

it may well be, but could all thirteen verses of the psalm be written on tablets so that one running past could read them? The vision is best taken as the words in 2:4–5, otherwise just the double statement in 2:4 (Driver): (1) that the puffed up (Babylonian), whose soul is not upright, (will be a casualty), but (2) the (Judahite) who is righteous will live by his faithfulness. The Hebrew word translated "faithfulness" can also mean "trustworthiness"; when referring to dealings in money it means "in honesty" (2 Kgs 12:15 [Heb 12:16] and 22:7).

The word "Moreover" beginning 2:5 suggests that this verse intends to expands upon the puffed up Babylonian whose soul is not upright. Driver, Roberts, and Achtemeier combine this verse with the woes in 2:6–19, but it is better taken with the present unit. The Babylonian king is a treacherous (cf. Isa 24:16b; Jer 12:1) and haughty warrior, having like Sheol an insatiable appetite (cf. Isa 5:14; Prov 27:20; 30:15–16), wanting to conquer one nation after the other. But in the end he will not survive. Habakkuk in 2:5b is receiving an answer to his question in 1:17. His response, directed to the Babylonian evildoers, comes in the woe oracles following.

## REFLECTION

1. Why do you think Habakkuk climbed to the top of the watchtower to await his answer from the Lord?

2. Faithfulness and trustworthiness are precious commodities. Give examples of when you found this to be true.

3. Is there a difference between having faith and being faithful, and if so, what does each term mean? Do New Testament texts in Rom 1:17; Gal 3:11; and Heb 10:37–39 accurately reflect what Habakkuk is saying?

4. Is there a good pride as well as a bad pride? If so, give examples of each.

# 13

# "BUT YAHWEH IS IN HIS HOLY TEMPLE" (2:6B-20)

> 2 ⁶ᵇ*Woe to one who heaps up what is not his own—*
>     *for how long?—*
>         *and makes himself heavy with pledges!*
> ⁷*Will not your debtors[1] suddenly arise*
>     *and wake up causing you to tremble?*
>         *then you will be spoils for him*
> ⁸*Because you have plundered many nations*
>     *all the remnant of the peoples will plunder you*
> *From human bloodshed and violence to the earth*
>     *town and all who live in it*
> ⁹*Woe to one who shaves off unjust profit for his house*

1. The Hebrew term comes from a verb meaning "to bite (off)," referring here to money lenders who "bite off" (excessive) interest on their loans. Some commentators therefore translate the term as "creditors." But Habakkuk is playing on the term, referring to *debtors* becoming creditors when the tables are turned and they get their revenge on those who have taken advantage of them.

> *to set his nest in a high place*
> *to escape from the reach of harm!*
> <sup>10</sup>*You have counseled shame to your house*
> *cutting off many peoples*
> *you have forfeited your life*
> <sup>11</sup>*For a stone from the wall will cry out*
> *and a beam from the woodwork will answer.*
> <sup>12</sup>*Woe to one who builds a city with bloodshed*
> *and establishes a town with iniquity!*
> <sup>13</sup>*Is it not, take note, from Yahweh of hosts*
> *that peoples labor only for fire*
> *and persons grow weary only for nothing?*
> <sup>14</sup>*For the earth will be filled*
> *with the knowledge of the glory of Yahweh*
> *as the waters cover the sea.*
> <sup>15</sup>*Woe to one who makes his neighbor drink*
> *adding your poison[2] and then making him drunk*
> *in order to look upon their nakedness!*
> <sup>16</sup>*You have filled yourself with disgrace instead of glory*
> *drink, you also, and show your uncircumcision!*
> *The cup of Yahweh's right hand*
> *will come around to you*
> *with disgrace upon your glory*
> <sup>17</sup>*For the violence done to Lebanon will cover you*
> *and the ruin of wild beasts they terrified*
> *From human bloodshed and violence to the earth*
> *town and all who live in it*
> <sup>18</sup>*What benefit is an idol*
> *when its maker has shaped it*
> *a cast image and teacher of lies?*
> *When the one who forms his formed thing trusts in it*
> *to make worthless dumb idols!*
> <sup>19</sup>*Woe to one who says to wood, "Awake"*
> *to a silent stone, "Arise"!*
> *can it teach?*

---

2. The MT cannot be correct; read either "adding its poison" or just "adding poison."

> *Look it is overlaid with gold and silver
> and there is no breath at all in it*
> <sup>20</sup>*But Yahweh is in his holy temple
> Keep silent before him all the earth!*

## RHETORIC AND COMPOSITION

The Hebrew Bible concludes the present unit with a section after 2:20, which is also the chapter division. It does not mark the beginning with a prior section. Sections occur also at the conclusions of 2:8, 11, 14, 17, and 18, and except for 2:17 occur prior to a subsequent woe.

This passage is introduced by the following prose add-on (RSV; NRSV; *pace* Roberts):

> <sup>6a</sup>Will not all of these take up a parable[3] against him and a mocking riddle against him, and will say:

The introduction suggests that the woes to follow are spoken by the nations against the Babylonians (Driver), but the speaker is more likely the prophet who is responding to Yahweh's vision in 2:4–5.

The passage contains a number of rhetorical figures. There are two oxymorons (Driver): in 2:10, where Nebuchadnezzar, having planned for the safety of his own house, has unwittingly counseled shame on it! and in 2:16, where the Babylonian king will have his fill of disgrace rather than glory. There are also rhetorical questions with answers in 2:7–8 and 19 (*hypophora*).[4] The litany of woes (*anaphora*) recalls Isaiah's litany of woes against Jerusalem in Isa 5:8–23. The ones here are the following:

---

3. More properly a "taunt-song" (Driver; cf. Isa 14:4a).
4. Lundbom, *Hebrew Prophets*, 193–94.

*Woe to one ...* (2:6)
*Woe to one ...* (2:9)
*Woe to one ...* (2:12)
*Woe to one ...* (2:15)
............ (2:18)
Woe to one ...

## MESSAGE

This prophecy contains five woes against Babylon and the Babylonian king. The "woe" (Heb *hôy*) while not an outright curse, was nevertheless a strong invective portending disaster, used often by the prophets, especially Isaiah (Amos 5:18; 6:1; Mic 2:1; Isa 5:8–23; 10:1; 28:1; 30:1; 31:1; 33:1; Zeph 2:5; 3:1; Nah 3:1; Jer 22:13; 23:1; Ezek 13:3, 18). The term appears to have had its origin in funeral laments (Jer 22:18).[5] We hear of woes spoken by Jesus in the New Testament (Matt 23:13–36). Hebrew has a similar word *'ôy*, which is sometimes an invective (Hos 7:13; 9:12) and sometimes a cry of lament (Mic 7:1; Isa 6:5; Jer 4:13, 31; 6:4; 10:19; 15:10; etc.).

Habakkuk's first woe is against one who is greedy and arrogant, doubtless the Babylonian king, now Nebuchadnezzar II after the Battle of Carchemish in 605 (see *Judah in the Seventh Century*), but with him other Chaldeans. Like a merciless oriental usurer heaping up goods taken in pledge, looked upon with great disfavor by Israelites (Deut 24:10–13), this plunderer of nations will one day be shaken when former debtors suddenly awake and force him to give up ill-gotten gains. Then he will become spoils for them. Nebuchadnezzar has plundered many nations, Assyria, Egypt, and the Philistines to name just a few of the most recent, but those remaining, says the prophet, will live to plunder

---

5. Clifford, "Use of *Hôy* in the Prophets," 459.

him (Isa 14:4–23). A case of the *lex talionis* (cf. Isa 14:2b; 33:1)! Under this king has occurred no small amount of human bloodshed and violence: it has been everywhere—in towns and against the people inhabiting them (Isa 14:3–11; Jer 50:23; 51:7, 20–24).

The second woe is against one who shaves off unjust profit for his own house, who sets his residence on high to keep himself from impending calamity. Setting one's nest like a bird on high is applied by Jeremiah and Obadiah to the Edomites (Jer 49:16; Obad 4), but Habakkuk is referring here to the Babylonians, specifically the Babylonian king who thinks he can escape the reach (lit. hand) of harm. The expression "shaving off unjust profit," meaning being greedy for (unjust) gain, occurs also in Jer 6:13; 8:10; Prov 1:19 and 15:27. Jeremiah uttered a woe against Jehoiakim for doing the same thing and said that as a result people would not be crying "woe" for him when he died (Jer 22:13–19).

Here, as so often happens, something has gone awry: the Babylonian king has unwittingly counseled shame on himself and his house (cf. Hos 8:4b; Jer 7:18–19). He has cut off many peoples, as Yahweh did to Israel at the hand of Hazael (cf. 2 Kgs 10:32), but his house will not stand. He will have forfeited his own life (cf. Prov 20:2b). The very stones of buildings he has built will cry out, and beams of the woodwork will answer to his injustices. Nabopolassar and Nebuchadnezzar II carried out a massive building program.[6]

The third woe is against one who builds cities and towns by bloodshed and iniquity, which refers again to the Babylonian king and his building up of conquered cities and towns at the expense of bloodshed and forced labor. Micah's most remembered prophecy was against rulers who built up Zion with bloodshed and wrongdoing (Mic

6. Lundbom, "Builders of Ancient Babylon."

3:9–12). Jeremiah uttered a woe against Jehoiakim for doing the same thing (Jer 22:13–17). Does not Yahweh of hosts say that such labor is only for an eventual burning of the cities, that people weary themselves for nothing (cf. Jer 51:58b)? Be on notice, O king and people of Babylon, that the earth will be filled with the knowledge of the glory of Yahweh, as the waters cover the sea (Num 14:21; Isa 11:9b).

The fourth woe is against one who makes his neighbor drink to become drunk, perhaps adding poison (Driver: fury) to the cup, in order to gaze upon his nakedness. Reference is again to Babylon's savage power, making helpless nations drink the cup of wrath so it can gaze upon them exposed and shamed (Jer 51:7). Ward says Israelites were modest by comparison, citing the (humorous) incident of a drunken Noah and his sons behavior in Gen 9:21–23. Isaiah's symbolic walking about the streets of Jerusalem naked or half naked to dramatize the fate of Egyptian captives and Ethiopian exiles would have been viewed as a gross indignity (Isa 20:2). Habakkuk says the same will happen to the king of Babylon when Yahweh passes to him the cup of wrath (Jer 25:26b; cf. Ps 75:8 [Heb 75:9]; Lam 4:21b; Nah 3:5b; Isa 51:17). He will drink and get drunk, and his exposed uncircumcision will bring him disgrace instead of glory (cf. Hos 4:7).

The Babylonian king is further judged for violence done to Lebanon, perhaps like the Assyrian kings, cutting cedar trees for interiors of temples and other buildings (Isa 14:8; cf. *ANET*[3] 275). This excess will eventually "clothe" him, as will his cruelty in hunting adventures. Babylonian kings, like their Assyrian predecessors, reveled in hunting wild beasts (Ward). One day the Babylonians will be visited by the beasts they terrified for all the bloodshed and violence done to the earth, in towns and against all inhabiting them. The fourth woe has a refrain-like ending similar to the first woe (2:8). Verse 18 belongs to the fifth woe.

The fifth woe begins by asking, what benefit is the idol after its maker has shaped it? Jeremiah said (Baal) "no-gods" profit nothing (Jer 2:8b, 11), that idols are nothings and instructors of nothing (Jer 10:8, 15). Idols are but cast images, and through priests are teachers of lies (cf. Jer 16:19b). The maker puts his trust in the worthless, dumb idols he creates (Isa 29:16b; 44:9–20; Ps 135:15–18; cf. 1 Cor 12:2). Idols are fastened so they cannot move and so they may not topple; they do not speak and have to be carried (Deut 4:28; Isa 40:20; 41:6–7; 46:6–7 Jer 10:3–5; Ps 115:5; WisSol 13:15–16; cf. 1 Sam 5:1–4). Moses told the Israelites that idols of wood and stone "neither see, nor hear, nor eat, nor smell" (Deut 4:28; cf. Ps 115:6). On idols of the Babylonians, see Isa 21:9b; Jer 50:38b. The two verses are here inverted so the woe comes second, bringing the series to a conclusion.

The final woe is against one who says "awake" to inert wood and "arise" to silent stones (cf. Jer 2:27–28). Can either teach? Can either rise up and give protection in a time of trouble (Deut 32:37–38; Jer 2:28; Isa 46:7)? Look at them: wood overlaid with gold and silver; there is no breath in them (Jer 10:3–5, 8–9, 14–15; Pss 115:4–8; 135:15–17; Isa 44:9–20; 46:6–7; 1 Cor 12:2).

Habakkuk closes with a marvelous confession having a dual function in structuring the core prophecy (see Prophets of the Seventh Century: Habakkuk, above):

> But Yahweh is in his holy temple
> Keep silent before him all the earth!

Yahweh is in his holy temple (Ps 11:4). On the call to be silent before Yahweh, see Ps 46:10 [Heb 46:11] and Zeph 1:7.

This concluding confession has survived in Christian worship where it often serves as a spoken or choral call to worship. George F. Root (1820–1895) immortalized the words in a musical arrangement used widely in a variety of liturgical contexts:[7]

> The LORD is in his holy temple
> The LORD is in is holy temple
> Let all the earth keep silence
> Let all the earth keep silence before Him
> Keep silence, Keep silence, before Him.
>                           Amen

With Chinese friends I attended Sunday morning worship at the large Fancheng church in central China on May 25, 2008, and heard the choir sing "The Lord is in his holy temple" in Chinese translation to the familiar melody as its call to worship[8]

## REFLECTION

1. How do we tell the difference between gaining profit and profiteering? Are people engaged in the latter eventually found out?

2. Can you think of an instance when you have unwittingly counseled your own shame? Has it happened to someone you know?

3. Do you think the Lord is saying even today that people weary themselves for nothing?

4. Have you heard "The Lord is in his holy temple" in Christian worship, and if so, what function did it have?

---

7. CovH #590.

8. For more on the worship service at the Fancheng church, at which over a thousand people were in attendance, see Lundbom, *On the Road to Siangyang*, 131–36.

# 14

# "YAHWEH THE LORD IS MY STRENGTH" (3:2–19)

3 ²*O Yahweh, I have heard report of you*
 *and I stand in awe, O Yahweh, of your work*
*In the midst of years revive it*
 *in the midst of years make it known*
  *in agitation remember mercy*
³*God comes from Teman*
 *and the Holy One from Mount Paran*
*His splendor covered the heavens*
 *and the earth was full of his praise*
⁴*And brightness as sunlight appears*
 *rays come forth from his hand*
  *and there is the hiding place of his might*
⁵*Before him goes pestilence*
 *and fire bolts go forth at his feet*
⁶*He stood still and measured the earth*
 *he looked and made the nations leap*
*The ancient mountains were shattered*
 *the everlasting hills were bowed down*

### Yahweh the Lord Is My Strength

*the everlasting ways are his*
⁷*Under affliction I saw the tents of Cushan*[1]
  *tent-curtains of the land of Midian were agitated*
⁸*Was wrath against rivers, O Yahweh?*
  *or your anger against the rivers*
    *or your fury against the sea*
*That you ride upon your horses*
  *your chariots of victory?*
⁹*Your naked bow is made bare*
  *oaths to arrows are decreed*
    *you break open the earth with rivers*
¹⁰*Mountains saw you and were in pangs*
  *a downpour of water swept by*
*The deep gave forth its voice*
  *it lifted its hands on high*
¹¹*Sun and moon stood still in their exalted place*
  *for light of your arrows go forth*
    *for brightness the glittering of your spear*
¹²*In indignation you march the earth*
  *in anger you trample nations*
¹³*You went forth for the salvation of your people*
  *for the salvation of your anointed one*
*You smote the head of the wicked house*
  *laying bare foundation to roof*
¹⁴*You pierced with his arrows the head of warriors*
  *who came as a whirlwind to scatter me*
    *their rejoicing as to devour the poor in hiding*
¹⁵*You trod the sea with your horses*
  *a heap of many waters*
¹⁶*I heard and was agitated within*
  *at the sound my lips quivered*
*Decay entered into my bones*
  *and my steps were agitated beneath me*
*That I must wait quietly for the day of distress*
  *to come upon the people who attack us*
¹⁷*For the fig tree does not bud*

---

1. Presumably a neighboring tribe to Midian.

*and no fruit is on the vines*
*The olive yield fails*
*and fields do not produce food*
*The flock is cut off from the fold*
*and there is no cattle in the stalls*
<sup>18</sup>*Yet I will exult in Yahweh*
*I will rejoice in the God of my salvation*
<sup>19</sup>*Yahweh[2] the Lord is my strength*
*and he makes my feet like the deer*
*and makes me tread upon my high places.*

## RHETORIC AND COMPOSITION

This is a psalm said to have been sung by Habakkuk. Ward says musical instruction in the subscription indicates that the psalm was intended for recitation in temple worship. In the Psalter provenance of a particular psalm and any musical instruction, when occurring together, are combined in a superscription (Psalms 5–9 and others). Here provenance and musical instruction are divided to form a superscription and subscription. The two read:

> 3 <sup>1</sup>*A prayer of Habakkuk the prophet according to Shigionoth[3]*
> ................
> ................
> 3 <sup>19b</sup>*To the choirmaster: with my stringed instruments*

The instruction "to the choirmaster" occurs in titles to fifty-four psalms (Driver). The present psalm may be a later addition to the book (Driver; Ward) as the Habakkuk scroll from Qumran does not contain it. But it may have been composed by the prophet (Roberts; Achtemeier). It is

---

2. M<sup>L</sup> mistakenly points the divine name "Yahweh."

3. An obscure musical term appearing in the singular in the superscription to Psalm 7.

well integrated into the book, especially with 3:16 supporting Yahweh's word to Habakkuk about *waiting for the vision* in 2:3, and the psalm's affirmation in 3:17–19 supporting Habakkuk's words about "the righteous living by his faithfulness" in 2:4. As for the psalm itself, the first-person narratives of 3:2 and 3:16–19 frame the intervening hymnic verses. Verses 3–15 may also connect directly to the woes in 2:6–20 (Achtemeier).

The composition sounds like many a biblical psalm with its parallelism and exaltation of Yahweh as God of creation (Pss 18:7–15; 29:3–10; 104; etc.) and worker of salvation (Pss 68:19–20; 74:12–17; 79:9; 85:4; etc.). It contains numerous repetitions (3:2, 6, 8, 13) with "in the midst of years" in v. 2 being anaphora.

## MESSAGE

This song with its quasi-mythological and historical imagery celebrates Yahweh and his mighty acts from hoary antiquity—against nations and for Israel's salvation. It contains only covert allusions to the defining events of Sinai and Canaan (Ward), the psalmist being more concerned about imminent distress. He nevertheless rejoices in the God of his salvation.

The psalmist begins by saying that he has heard report of Yahweh and stands in awe of his great work. Would that after many years Yahweh might revive it and make it known, but amidst all the agitation may Yahweh nevertheless remember mercy.

The prophet recalls in a vision following that in hoary antiquity Israel's God resided on two mountains in the southern wilderness, one in Edomite Teman, the other in the Wilderness of Paran (cf. Exod 18:1–12). The tradition is given fuller explanation in Deuteronomy's prologue to the

Blessing of Moses (Deut 33:2–5), where a third mountain is added, namely Sinai (or Horeb), the mountain of record in Israel's salvation history where Yahweh covenanted with Israel (Deut 5:2–3). Instead of Teman the site in Deut 33:2, as in Judg 5:4, is Seir, another name for the land of Edom. Mount Seir—or the Seir mountain range—is located in Edomite territory west of the Arabah (Gen 36:8–9), receiving mention in the Amarna Letters (*ANET*³ 488) and in Egyptian texts of Ramses II (ca. 1290–224) and Ramses III (ca. 1183–1152).[4] The prologue to the Blessing of Moses goes on to say that Yahweh left behind thousands of adoring holy ones on these mountains to throw in his lot with "peoples," specifically the people of Israel over whom he would become King (Deut 33:5).[5]

Yahweh's splendor covered the heavens, and the earth was full of his praise. His brightness appeared as the full light of the sun (Driver; cf. Job 31:26). Rays (lit. horns) of lightning came forth from his hand, or from his side. Roberts points out that ANE storm gods were typically portrayed with stylized lightning bolts in their hand (cf. *ANEP*² 490, 500, 501, 531, 532). But with Yahweh's brightness appearing as sunlight, the rays were perhaps coming "from his side" (Driver). Ward says Babylonian art often represented solar deities with rays proceeding from the body (cf. *ANEP*² 498). In any case, behind the brightness and rays lie hidden the fullness of Israel's God.

Yahweh's personified attendants are pestilence (Lev 26:25) and fire bolts, or fiery darts (Ps 76:3; Song 8:6), where the Hebrew term *resheph* ("fire-bolts") recalls the fire or lightning god Resheph worshiped in Syria, Phoenicia, Egypt, and Cyprus.[6] Resheph appears in Akkadian and

4. Aharoni, *Land of the Bible*, 182.
5. Lundbom, *Deuteronomy*, 919–24.
6. Handy, "Resheph" in *ABD* 5:678–79.

Ugaritic texts, and is attested also at Ebla. Fire bolts bring pestilence, burning fever, and death (cf. Deut 32:24: "eaten up with the fire-bolt"; RSV: "devoured with burning heat"; NRSV: "burning consumption").

Yahweh stood still and surveyed the earth; he looked and nations leaped in fright. Ancient mountains were shattered and primeval hills bowed low. The ways of Yahweh—like the immovable mountains and hills—are old and belong to him. The psalmist recalls that at the exodus Midianites and neighboring tribes quaked with fear (Num 31:7–8; Judg 3:9–10; cf. Exod 15:14–16). Was the divine wrath against the rivers or the sea when Yahweh rode to victory? Horses and chariots rumbled on storm clouds ridden by Yahweh (Pss 18:10–15; 68:33; 104:3; Deut 33:26). Verse 9 is particularly difficult. The idea seems to be that with Yahweh's bow out from its covering and its arrows decreed by oath, the earth is broken open yielding rivers. Mountains were in pangs at the display of the divine power, with water pouring from above and waters of the deep roaring loudly (cf. Ps 77:16–17). Sun and moon stood still in their respective abodes, hidden by dark clouds (cf. Ps 19:4b–5); nevertheless, the light of Yahweh's arrows and brightness of his spear lit up heaven and earth. In indignation Yahweh marched the earth and trampled nations (cf. Ps 77:16–18).

Was this show of divine power only against the nations? No, it was to save the anointed one, which could be a (future) Davidic king (Achtemeier; cf. Jer 23:5–6) or all Israel. The psalmist returns to describe effects of divine power on the enemy. Yahweh smote the house of the wicked, laying it bare from foundation to roof. Arrows taken from the enemy were used to pierce heads of warriors who saw the whirlwind scattering them like chaff. The first-person "me" refers to the people in whose name the words were spoken (Driver). But the warriors' elation after plundering the helpless poor in some secret place was short-lived (cf. Ps 10:8–9). Yahweh trod the sea with horses, making waters rise in a heap (Ps 77:19). Driver says this may refer to the ruin of Egyptians at the Red Sea (Exod 15:1–16), although here is no destruction of any foe.

The psalmist has heard this (cf. 3:2), and his innards were in turmoil (cf. Jer 4:19); his lips quivered at the sound. Even his bones were affected; so unsteady was he of foot that he could barely walk. Nevertheless, he must wait quietly for distress to fall upon those attacking Judah (cf. 2:3), who were the Babylonians (Achtemeier). Even though the fig tree does not bud, no fruit hangs on the grapevines, olives fail on the olive trees, fields do not produce grain, sheep are cut off from the fold, no cattle can be seen in the stalls, the psalmist will nevertheless exalt in Yahweh the God of his salvation (cf. Mic 7:7). Achtemeier sees here a possible comparison to Jer 5:17, in which case Habakkuk fears an invasion by the Babylonians in 600, just two years before Nebuchadnezzar actually besieged Jerusalem and the next year forced its surrender. Yahweh, nevertheless, is the psalmist's strength, making his feet like those of a deer and enabling him to trod the heights (cf. 2 Sam 22:34; Ps 18:33 [Heb 18:34]).

## REFLECTION

1. Having heard about God's mighty acts in years past, do you ever pray that God will do the same today? If so, what sort of mighty acts would you ask for?

2. The Lord is gracious and merciful, forgiving iniquity, transgression, and sin, but do you agree that he will by no means clear the guilty (Exod 34:6–7)? In the New Testament, see Paul's words in Rom 2:4–11.

3. Is the quasi-mythological poetry in 3:3–15 of any value today as we think about the greatness and might of God? Might we add insights gained from modern science?
4. Can we say with Habakkuk that even though enemy forces are clearly at work in the world, we can nevertheless exult in the Lord and rejoice in the God of our salvation?

# BIBLIOGRAPHY

Achtemeier, Elizabeth. *Nahum–Malachi*. Interpretation. Atlanta: John Knox, 1986.
Aharoni, Yohanan. *The Land of the Bible*. Translated and edited by A. F. Rainey. 2nd ed., rev. and enl. Philadelphia: Westminster, 1979.
Berlin, Adele. *Zephaniah*. AB 25A. New York: Doubleday, 1994.
Bright, John. *A History of Israel*. 3rd ed. Westminster Aids to the Study of the Scriptures. Philadelphia: Westminster, 1981.
Brinkman, J. A. *Prelude to Empire: Babylonian Society and Politics 747–626 B.C.* Occasional Publications of the Babylonian Fund 7. Philadelphia: Distributed by the Babylonian Fund. University Museum, 1984.
Cathcart, Kevin J. "Nahum, Book of." In *ABD* 4:998–1000.
Cathcart, Kevin J., and Robert P. Gordon. *The Targum to the Minor Prophets*. AramB 14. Wilmington, DE: Glazier, 1989.
Clifford, Richard J. "The Use of Hôy in the Prophets." *CBQ* 28 (1966) 458–64.
Driver, S. R. ed. *The Minor Prophets II: Nahum, Habakkuk, Zephaniah, Haggai, Zechariah, Malachi*. Century Bible. Edinburgh: Jack, 1906.
Ego, Beate, et al., eds. *Biblia Qumranica*. Vol 3B. *Minor Prophets*. Leiden: Brill, 2005.
Eissfeldt, Otto. *The Old Testament: An Introduction*. Translated by Peter R. Ackroyd. New York: Harper & Row, 1965.
Ginsburg, Christian D. *Introduction to the Massoretico-Critical Edition of the Hebrew Bible*. 1897. Reprint, New York: Ktav, 1966.
Haak, Robert D. *Habakkuk*. VTSup 44. Leiden: Brill, 1992.
Handy, Lowell K. "Resheph." In *ABD* 5:678–79.

*Bibliography*

Herodotus. *Herodotus I: Books 1–2*. Translated by A. D. Godley. LCL. Cambridge: Harvard University Press, 1966.
Heschel, Abraham. *The Prophets*. New York: Harper & Row, 1962.
Josephus, Flavius. *Josephus VI: Jewish Antiquities: Books 9–11*. Translated by Ralph Marcus. LCL. Cambridge: Harvard University Press, 1966.
Lundbom, Jack R. "Builders of Ancient Babylon: Nabopolassar and Nebuchadnezzar II." *Int* 71 (2017) 154–66.
———. *Deuteronomy: A Commentary*. Grand Rapids; Eerdmans, 2013.
———. *The Hebrew Prophets: An Introduction*. Minneapolis: Fortress, 2010.
———. "Jeremiah as Covenant Mediator." In *The Book of Jeremiah: Composition, Reception, and Interpretation*, edited by Jack R. Lundbom et al., 437–54. Formation and Interpretation of Old Testament Literature. VTSup 178. Leiden: Brill, 2018.
———. *Jeremiah 1–20*. AB 21A. New York: Doubleday / New Haven: Yale University Press, 1999.
———. *Jeremiah 21–36*. AB 21B. New York: Doubleday / New Haven: Yale University Press, 2004.
———. *Jeremiah 37–52* AB 21C. New York: Doubleday / New Haven: Yale University Press, 2004.
———. "The Lawbook of the Josianic Reform." *CBQ* 38 (1976) 293–302.
———. *On the Road to Siangyang: Covenant Mission in Mainland China 1890–1949*. Eugene, OR: Pickwick Publications, 2015.
———. "Prophets in the Hebrew Bible." In *The Oxford Research Encyclopedia of Religion*, edited by John Barton. New York: Oxford University, 2016. http://religion.oxfordre.com/.
———. "Rhetorical Structures in Jeremiah 1." *ZAW* 103 (1991) 193–210.
Luther, Martin. *Lectures on the Minor Prophets I*. Luther's Works 18. Edited by Hilton C. Oswald. St. Louis: Concordia, 1975.
Muilenburg, James. "Old Testament Prophecy." In *Peake's Commentary on the Bible*, edited by Mathew Black and H. H. Rowley, 475–83. London: Nelson, 1977.
———. "A Study in Hebrew Rhetoric: Repetition and Style." In *Congress Volume, Copenhagen, 1953*, 97–111. VTSup 1. Leiden: Brill, 1953.
Rad, Gerhard von. "The Origin of the Concept of the Day of Yahweh." *JSS* 4 (1959) 97–108.

*Bibliography*

Roberts, J. J. M. *Nahum, Habakkuk, and Zephaniah: A Commentary.* OTL. Louisville: Westminster John Knox, 1991.

Robinson, H. Wheeler. "Prophetic Symbolism." In *Old Testament Essays*, edited by D. C. Simpson, 1–17. London: Griffin, 1927.

Smith, J. M. Powis. "Nahum." In *A Critical and Exegetical Commentary on Micah, Zephaniah, Nahum, Habakkuk, Obadiah and Joel*, edited by J. M. Powis Smith et al., 267–360. ICC. Edinburgh: T. & T. Clark, 1911.

———. "Zephaniah." In *A Critical and Exegetical Commentary on Micah, Zephaniah, Nahum, Habakkuk, Obadiah and Joel*, edited by J. M. Powis Smith et al., 159–263. ICC. Edinburgh: T. & T. Clark, 1911.

Ward, William Hayes. "Habakkuk." In *A Critical and Exegetical Commentary on Micah, Zephaniah, Nahum, Habakkuk, Obadiah and Joel*, edited by J. M. Powis Smith et al., 3–28. Edinburgh: T. & T. Clark, 1911.

Wiseman, D. J. "Assyrian Writing-Boards." *Iraq* 17 (1955) 3–13.

# NAME INDEX

Achtemeier, Elizabeth, 87, 91, 114, 117, 118, 130, 131, 133, 134
Aharoni, Yohanan, 132
Augustine, Saint, 10

Berlin, Adele, 49, 54, 59
Bright, John, 3
Brinkman, J. A., 6
Bush, George H. W., 9

Clifford, Richard J., 123

Driver, S. R., 14, 45, 46, 47, 50, 51, 53, 54, 80, 84, 87, 91, 95, 101, 102, 110, 115, 116, 117, 118, 122, 125, 130, 132, 133, 134

Eissfeldt, Otto, 10

Ginsburg, Christian D., 110
Gorbachev, Mikhail, 9

Haak, Robert, 20
Handy, Lowell K., 132
Heschel, Abraham, 11, 12, 13, 41, 82, 84, 96

Johnson, Douglas, xi

Lundbom, Jack R., 5, 21, 22, 25, 28, 33, 46, 51, 76, 92, 93. 122, 124, 127, 132
Luther, Martin, 116

MacArthur, Douglas, 9
Muilenburg, James, 49

Rad, Gerhard von, 51
Roberts, J. J. M., 60, 74, 80, 82, 83, 84, 87, 91, 94, 98, 110, 111, 113, 115, 116, 117, 118, 122, 130, 132
Root, George F., 126

Sargent, John Singer, 54
Smith, J. M. Powis, 48, 66, 80, 102, 104, 115

Ward, William Hayes, 125, 130, 131, 132
Wiseman, D. J. 117

# SCRIPTURE INDEX

## OLD TESTAMENT

### Genesis
| | |
|---|---|
| 6:7 | 52 |
| 7:4 | 52 |
| 8:8 | 52 |
| 9:21–23 | 125 |
| 10:6 | 98 |
| 18:16—19:29 | 62 |
| 25:22–23 | 52 |
| 36:8–9 | 132 |

### Exodus
| | |
|---|---|
| 3:7–22 | 35 |
| 9:27 | 68 |
| 14:2 | 83 |
| 14:9 | 83 |
| 15:1–16 | 134 |
| 15:14–16 | 133 |
| 15:19b | 83 |
| 18:1–12 | 131 |
| 18:15 | 52 |
| 19:16–19 | 35 |
| 20:4–6 | 88 |
| 20:5 | 81, 82 |
| 20:18–19 | 35 |
| 32:11–14 | 35 |
| 32:30–32 | 35 |
| 33:1–17 | 35 |
| 34:6–7 | 82–83, 134 |
| 34:6 | 12 |
| 34:14 | 81 |

### Leviticus
| | |
|---|---|
| 10:10 | 67 |
| 19:18 | 82 |
| 26:25 | 132 |

### Numbers
| | |
|---|---|
| 11:1–3 | 35 |
| 13–14 | 36 |
| 13:29 | 61 |
| 14:14 | 74 |
| 14:18 | 12, 83 |
| 14:21 | 125 |
| 16 | 36 |
| 31:7–8 | 133 |

### Deuteronomy
| | |
|---|---|
| 1:26–46 | 36 |
| 2:23 | 61 |
| 4:3 | 51 |

## Deuteronomy (*cont.*)

| | |
|---|---|
| 4:9–14 | 35 |
| 4:19 | 46, 52 |
| 4:24 | 55, 81 |
| 4:28 | 126 |
| 4:29 | 53 |
| 4:32–40 | 35 |
| 4:37 | 85 |
| 5:2–5 | 35 |
| 5:2–3 | 132 |
| 5:8–10 | 88 |
| 5:22–27 | 35 |
| 6:13 | 52 |
| 6:15 | 81 |
| 7:4 | 51 |
| 7:7–8 | 85 |
| 9:7–21 | 35 |
| 9:22–29 | 35 |
| 10:10–11 | 35 |
| 10:15 | 85 |
| 10:20 | 52 |
| 11:14–15 | 51 |
| 16:1–17 | 75, 94 |
| 17:3 | 46, 51, 52 |
| 17:8–12 | 68 |
| 18:18 | 27 |
| 21:5 | 68 |
| 23:21–23 | 94 |
| 24:10–13 | 123 |
| 26:19 | 75 |
| 27:2–8 | 117 |
| 28:20 | 51 |
| 28:28–29 | 55 |
| 28:30 | 55 |
| 28:39 | 55 |
| 28:68 | 51 |
| 29:5–6 | 51 |
| 29:22 [Heb] | 62 |
| 29:23 | 62 |
| 32 | 75 |
| 32:4 | 68, 113 |
| 32:15 | 113 |
| 32:18 | 113 |
| 32:21 | 82 |
| 32:24 | 133 |
| 32:30 | 113 |
| 32:32 | 62 |
| 32:37–38 | 126 |
| 33:2–5 | 132 |
| 33:2 | 132 |
| 33:5 | 132 |
| 33:10 | 68 |
| 33:26 | 133 |

## Joshua

| | |
|---|---|
| 4:22–23 | 83 |
| 13:3 | 61 |

## Judges

| | |
|---|---|
| 3:9–10 | 133 |
| 5:4 | 132 |
| 5:22 | 101 |
| 15:19 | 47 |

## Ruth

| | |
|---|---|
| 3:14—4:12 | 68 |

## 1 Samuel

| | |
|---|---|
| 3 | 27 |
| 5:1–4 | 126 |
| 5:4–5 | 46 |
| 5:5 | 54 |
| 7:7–11 | 36 |
| 8:4–9 | 36 |
| 12:7–25 | 36 |
| 30:14 | 61 |

## 2 Samuel

| | |
|---|---|
| 4:5 | 61 |
| 12:16 | 52 |

| | | | |
|---|---|---|---|
| 18:24–27 | 116 | 19:1–36 | 21 |
| 21:1 | 52 | 19:4 | 96 |
| 22:34 | 134 | 19:9 | 96 |
| | | 19:14 | 96 |
| **1 Kings** | | 19:23 | 96 |
| 7:16–17 | 5 | 19:35–37 | 3 |
| 11:5 | 46 | 21:1–21 | 4 |
| 11:33 | 46 | 21:1–15 | 88 |
| 14:5 | 53 | 21:3 | 46, 52 |
| 17:7 | 83 | 21:5 | 46, 52 |
| 19:11a | 84 | 21:18 | 39 |
| 20:16 | 61 | 21:19–24 | 39 |
| 22:5–8 | 53 | 21:23–24 | 4 |
| 22:17 | 104 | 21:24 | 39 |
| | | 22:1 | 53 |
| **2 Kings** | | 22:3—23:3 | 15 |
| | | 22:3–20 | 27 |
| 1:2 | 51 | 22:3–13 | 5, 39 |
| 1:10 | 84 | 22:7 | 118 |
| 1:12 | 84 | 22:14–20 | 6, 38, 39 |
| 8:12 | 102 | 22:14 | 47, 54 |
| 9:17 | 116 | 23:1–3 | 6, 39 |
| 10:22 | 53 | 23:4–20 | 5, 39 |
| 10:32 | 124 | 23:5 | 52 |
| 12:15 | 118 | 23:12 | 52 |
| 12:16 [Heb] | 118 | 23:13 | 46 |
| 15:29 | 2, 102 | 23:21–23 | 6, 15, 39 |
| 16 | 2 | 23:24 | 5, 39 |
| 16:7 | 96 | 23:26 | 4 |
| 17:3–6 | 2 | 23:29–30 | 7, 40 |
| 17:6 | 102 | 23:30 | 53 |
| 17:24 | 2 | 23:31 | 53 |
| 18:3–6 | 3 | 23:31–33 | 40 |
| 18:3 | 14 | 23:32 | 53 |
| 18:4–7 | 14 | 23:34 | 53 |
| 18:7 | 3 | 23:34a | 40 |
| 18:11 | 102 | 23:34b | 40 |
| 18:13–35 | 82 | 23:36 | 53 |
| 18:13 | 3, 102 | 24:1 | 8, 40, 41 |
| 18:17 | 96 | 24:3–4 | 4 |
| 19 | 73 | 24:6 | 8, 41 |

## 2 Kings (*cont.*)

| | |
|---|---|
| 24:8 | 41 |
| 24:10–16 | 8 |
| 24:10–11 | 41 |
| 24:12–16 | 41 |
| 24:17 | 8, 41 |
| 24:29–30 | 94 |
| 24:37 | 53 |

## 2 Chronicles

| | |
|---|---|
| 16:10 | 31 |
| 26:15 | 48 |
| 28:2 | 88 |
| 29–31 | 3 |
| 33:10–20 | 4 |
| 33:14 | 54 |
| 33:20 | 39 |
| 33:21–25 | 39 |
| 34:1 | 39 |
| 34:3a | 39 |
| 34:3b-7 | 5, 39 |
| 34:3b | 5, 14 |
| 34:8–21 | 5, 39 |
| 34:22–28 | 39, 56 |
| 34:29–33 | 39 |
| 35:1–19 | 6, 39 |
| 35:20–24 | 7, 40, 94 |
| 35:22 | 28 |
| 35:25 | 28, 40 |
| 36:1–3 | 40 |
| 36:4a | 40 |
| 36:4b | 40 |
| 36:5 | 53 |
| 36:6 | 41 |
| 36:7 | 41 |
| 36:9–10a | 41 |
| 36:10 | 41 |
| 36:15 | 68 |

## Nehemiah

| | |
|---|---|
| 3:3 | 54 |
| 12:39 | 54 |
| 13:16 | 54 |

## Job

| | |
|---|---|
| 18:18 | 84 |
| 19:7 | 112 |
| 31:26 | 132 |

## Psalms

| | |
|---|---|
| 5–9 | 130 |
| 5:3 | 117 |
| 5:4 [Heb] | 117 |
| 7 | 130 |
| 10:1 | 112 |
| 10:7 | 112 |
| 10:8–9 | 134 |
| 11:4 | 126 |
| 11:4a | 24 |
| 11:10 | 68 |
| 12:5 | 74 |
| 12:6 [Heb] | 74 |
| 18:2 | 113 |
| 18:3 [Heb] | 113 |
| 18:6 | 112 |
| 18:7 | 83 |
| 18:10–15 | 133 |
| 18:27 | 74 |
| 18:28 [Heb] | 74 |
| 18:31 | 113 |
| 18:32 [Heb] | 113 |
| 18:33 | 134 |
| 18:34 [Heb] | 134 |
| 18:46 | 113 |
| 18:47 [Heb] | 113 |
| 19:4b-5 | 133 |
| 19:14 | 113 |
| 19:15 [Heb] | 113 |
| 22:1 | 112 |

## Scripture Index

| | |
|---|---|
| 22:2 [Heb] | 112 |
| 23:3 | 73 |
| 23:5 | 73 |
| 24:6 | 53 |
| 27:14 | 73 |
| 28:1 | 113 |
| 29:5 | 83 |
| 31:24 | 73 |
| 35:10 | 74 |
| 37:6 | 68 |
| 37:39 | 84 |
| 46:10 | 126 |
| 46:11 [Heb] | 126 |
| 47:4 | 95 |
| 60:3 | 103 |
| 60:5 [Heb] | 103 |
| 66:6 | 83 |
| 68:29 | 74 |
| 68:30 [Heb] | 74 |
| 68:33 | 133 |
| 69:23 | 95 |
| 74:1 | 112 |
| 74:15 | 83 |
| 75:8 | 125 |
| 75:9 [Heb] | 125 |
| 76:3 | 132 |
| 76:11 | 74 |
| 76:12 [Heb] | 74 |
| 77:16–18 | 133 |
| 77:16–17 | 133 |
| 77:19 | 83, 134 |
| 77:20 [Heb] | 83 |
| 79:5 | 55 |
| 86:15 | 83 |
| 101:8 | 68 |
| 103:9 | 82 |
| 104:3 | 133 |
| 105:3–4 | 53 |
| 106:9 | 83 |
| 115:4–8 | 126 |
| 115:5 | 126 |
| 115:6 | 126 |
| 118:8–9 | 74 |
| 135:15–18 | 126 |
| 135:15–17 | 126 |
| 137:9 | 103 |

### Proverbs

| | |
|---|---|
| 1:2–3 | 67 |
| 1:7–8 | 67 |
| 1:7 | 68 |
| 1:19 | 124 |
| 3:11 | 67 |
| 4:1 | 67 |
| 4:13 | 67 |
| 5:12 | 67 |
| 5:23 | 67 |
| 6:6–7 | 114 |
| 6:26 | 101 |
| 7:10–23 | 101 |
| 9:10 | 68 |
| 15:27 | 124 |
| 16:18 | 62 |
| 20:2b | 124 |
| 22:24 | 82 |
| 27:20 | 118 |
| 27:22 | 47 |
| 28:14 | 67 |
| 29:22 | 82 |
| 30:15–16 | 118 |
| 30:27 | 114 |

### Ecclesiastes

| | |
|---|---|
| 9:12 | 114 |

### Song of Songs

| | |
|---|---|
| 8:6 | 132 |

### Isaiah

| | |
|---|---|
| 1:4–9 | 102 |

## Isaiah (*cont.*)

| Reference | Page |
|---|---|
| 1:4 | 113 |
| 1:9–10 | 62 |
| 1:23 | 67 |
| 1:24 | 82 |
| 1:25–27 | 14, 74 |
| 2:7 | 102 |
| 2:13 | 83 |
| 3:14 | 67 |
| 4:3–6 | 14 |
| 4:3 | 74 |
| 5:8–23 | 122, 123 |
| 5:8–10 | 67 |
| 5:14 | 118 |
| 5:19 | 113 |
| 5:23 | 67 |
| 5:24 | 113 |
| 6:5–7 | 74 |
| 6:5 | 123 |
| 8:1 | 117 |
| 8:5–8 | 84 |
| 8:16–17 | 3 |
| 8:17 | 23, 73 |
| 8:22 | 55 |
| 9:2–7 | 3 |
| 9:5 [Heb] | 75 |
| 9:6 | 75 |
| 10:1 | 123 |
| 10:2 | 67 |
| 10:22 | 74 |
| 10:24–27 | 87 |
| 11:1–9 | 3 |
| 11:9b | 125 |
| 11:11 | 74 |
| 11:14 | 62 |
| 12:6 | 74–75 |
| 13:6 | 51, 53 |
| 13:10 | 55 |
| 13:16 | 102 |
| 13:19 | 62 |
| 14:2b | 124 |
| 14:3–11 | 124 |
| 14:4–23 | 124 |
| 14:4a | 122 |
| 14:8 | 125 |
| 14:25b | 87 |
| 14:30 | 74 |
| 14:32 | 74 |
| 16:6 | 62 |
| 18:1–2 | 74 |
| 18:7 | 74 |
| 19:5 | 102 |
| 19:16 | 103 |
| 20 | 61 |
| 20:2 | 125 |
| 21:6–9 | 117 |
| 21:9b | 126 |
| 23:8 | 54 |
| 24:16b | 118 |
| 25:4 | 74 |
| 26:8 | 73 |
| 26:20 | 61 |
| 28:1 | 123 |
| 28:5–6 | 14 |
| 28:7 | 67 |
| 29:6 | 83 |
| 29:16b | 126 |
| 29:19 | 74 |
| 30:1 | 123 |
| 30:8 | 117 |
| 30:9 | 67 |
| 30:18 | 23, 73 |
| 30:19–26 | 14 |
| 30:27–33 | 14 |
| 31:1 | 123 |
| 31:8–9 | 14 |
| 32:16–19 | 14 |
| 33:1 | 123, 124 |
| 33:2 | 73 |
| 33:9 | 83 |
| 35:2 | 83 |
| 36:1–20 | 82 |

## Scripture Index

| | | | |
|---|---|---|---|
| 40:7 | 83 | 1:10 | 34 |
| 40:20 | 126 | 1:12 | 27 |
| 41:6–7 | 126 | 1:13–19 | 21, 27, 39 |
| 41:23–24 | 54 | 1:13–16 | 27 |
| 42:13 | 75, 82 | 1:18 | 34 |
| 44:9–20 | 126 | 1:19 | 34 |
| 44:27 | 83 | 2:1—4:4 | 28 |
| 46:6–7 | 126 | 2:3 | 52, 60 |
| 46:7 | 126 | 2:8 | 68 |
| 47:9b | 101 | 2:8b | 126 |
| 49:13 | 74 | 2:9 | 60 |
| 50:2b | 83 | 2:11 | 126 |
| 51:10 | 83 | 2:12 | 60 |
| 51:17 | 125 | 2:15 | 68 |
| 51:19 | 101, 102 | 2:18 | 54 |
| 51:20 | 102 | 2:19 | 60 |
| 52:7 | 93 | 2:20 | 88 |
| 52:10 | 75 | 2:22 | 60 |
| 52:17–18 | 103 | 2:23 | 5 |
| 54:1 | 74 | 2:27–28 | 126 |
| 55:6 | 61, 63 | 2:28 | 126 |
| 56:10 | 117 | 2:29 | 60 |
| 58:2 | 61 | 2:30 | 67 |
| 59:9–10 | 55 | 3:1–5 | 92 |
| 59:17 | 82 | 3:1 | 60 |
| 61:2 | 82 | 3:5 | 82 |
| 62:5 | 75 | 3:6–11 | 27 |
| 63:14 | 82 | 3:10 | 60 |
| 64:4 | 73 | 3:12–18 | 28 |
| 65:19 | 75 | 3:12 | 60 |
| 65:21 | 55 | 3:13 | 60 |
| | | 3:14 | 60 |
| | | 3:16 | 60 |

### Jeremiah

| | | | |
|---|---|---|---|
| | | 3:20 | 60 |
| 1–20 | 28, 29 | 3:21–25 | 36 |
| 1:2 | 39 | 3:24–25 | 36 |
| 1:4–12 | 39 | 4:1–4 | 52 |
| 1:4 | 34 | 4:1 | 60 |
| 1:5 | 28 | 4:5—9:22 | 28 |
| 1:7 | 60 | 4:5–21 | 21 |
| 1:9–10 | 27 | 4:5–8 | 113 |
| 1:9 | 27 | | |

## Jeremiah (*cont.*)

| | |
|---|---|
| 4:7 | 61, 68 |
| 4:9 | 51, 53, 60 |
| 4:11–12 | 83 |
| 4:13 | 113, 123 |
| 4:17 | 67 |
| 4:19 | 134 |
| 4:23–31 | 21 |
| 4:23–26 | 52 |
| 4:24–25 | 83 |
| 4:29 | 61 |
| 4:31 | 123 |
| 5:1–19 | 21 |
| 5:1–9 | 50, 54, 67 |
| 5:1 | 112 |
| 5:3 | 67 |
| 5:4–5 | 54 |
| 5:5 | 88 |
| 5:6 | 113 |
| 5:15 | 113 |
| 5:17 | 134 |
| 5:23 | 67 |
| 5:28 | 112 |
| 5:30–31 | 68 |
| 6:1–12 | 21 |
| 6:4–5 | 51 |
| 6:4 | 123 |
| 6:4a | 61 |
| 6:13–15 | 112 |
| 6:13 | 68, 124 |
| 6:17 | 117 |
| 6:22–26 | 21 |
| 6:22–23 | 113 |
| 7:3–14 | 29, 40 |
| 7:3–7 | 61 |
| 7:6 | 67 |
| 7:8–11 | 92 |
| 7:9 | 51 |
| 7:13 | 68 |
| 7:16 | 37 |
| 7:18–19 | 124 |
| 7:18 | 46 |
| 7:20 | 84 |
| 7:23–26 | 67 |
| 7:25 | 68 |
| 7:28 | 67 |
| 8:1–2 | 46 |
| 8:2 | 52 |
| 8:7b | 61 |
| 8:7c | 112 |
| 8:10 | 124 |
| 9:10–11 [Heb] | 68 |
| 9:10 [Heb] | 61 |
| 9:11–12 | 68 |
| 9:11 | 61 |
| 9:21 [Heb] | 28, 104 |
| 9:22 | 104 |
| 9:24–25 [Heb] | 34 |
| 9:24 [Heb] | 54 |
| 9:25–26 | 34 |
| 9:25 | 54 |
| 10:3–5 | 126 |
| 10:5 | 15, 54 |
| 10:8–9 | 126 |
| 10:8 | 126 |
| 10:10 | 84 |
| 10:14–15 | 126 |
| 10:15 | 126 |
| 10:17–22 | 28 |
| 10:19 | 123 |
| 10:25 | 34 |
| 11:4 | 67 |
| 11:7–8 | 67 |
| 11:7 | 68 |
| 11:14 | 37 |
| 11:18—12:6 | 26 |
| 11:18–27 | 30 |
| 11:20 | 28, 82 |
| 11:22 | 54 |
| 12:1–2 | 112, 117 |
| 12:1 | 68, 114, 118 |

## Scripture Index

| | | | |
|---|---|---|---|
| 12:3 | 51 | 17:2–3 | 67 |
| 12:5–6 | 30 | 17:16 | 51 |
| 12:6 | 68 | 18:16 | 63 |
| 13:1–11 | 26, 117 | 18:17 | 83 |
| 13:12–14 | 26 | 18:18 | 36, 68 |
| 13:16 | 55 | 18:19–23 | 30, 36 |
| 13:18–20 | 30, 41 | 19:1—20:6 | 26 |
| 13:21 | 54 | 19:1–13 | 26, 30, 117 |
| 13:22 | 101 | | |
| 13:23 | 59 | 19:8 | 104 |
| 13:24 | 83 | 19:13 | 52 |
| 13:26 | 100, 101 | 19:14—20:6 | 31 |
| 14:1–6 | 36 | 20:7–10 | 31 |
| 14:7–9 | 36 | 20:8 | 112 |
| 14:9 | 75 | 20:11–13 | 31 |
| 14:10 | 36 | 20:11 | 75 |
| 14:11 | 37 | 20:14–18 | 31 |
| 14:13–14 | 67 | 20:18 | 28 |
| 14:15–16 | 36 | 21:1—23:8 | 26 |
| 14:17–19b | 37 | 21:1–7 | 37 |
| 14:18b | 68 | 21:1–2 | 26 |
| 14:19–22 | 37 | 21:3–7 | 26 |
| 14:20–22 | 36 | 21:12 | 68 |
| 15:1–3 | 37 | 22:1–5 | 26 |
| 15:1 | 36 | 22:3 | 67 |
| 15:4 | 4 | 22:13–19 | 22, 53, 124 |
| 15:5 | 101, 102 | | |
| 15:8 | 61 | 22:13–17 | 125 |
| 15:10 | 30, 123 | 22:13 | 123 |
| 15:15 | 30 | 22:18–19 | 8, 41 |
| 15:16 | 27, 39 | 22:18 | 123 |
| 15:18 | 112 | 22:21 | 67 |
| 15:20–21 | 30, 34 | 23:1 | 123 |
| 16:1–4 | 26 | 23:5–8 | 33 |
| 16:5–7 | 26 | 23:5–6 | 133 |
| 16:8–9 | 26 | 23:9–40 | 26 |
| 16:14–15 | 33 | 23:14 | 62 |
| 16:16 | 114 | 23:16–17 | 67 |
| 16:19–21 | 33 | 23:29 | 84 |
| 16:19 | 84 | 23:32 | 67 |
| 16:19b | 126 | 23:33–40 | 111 |

## Jeremiah (cont.)

| | |
|---|---|
| 24 | 31 |
| 25:3 | 68 |
| 25:4 | 68 |
| 25:11–14 | 22 |
| 25:12–15 | 26 |
| 25:15–29 | 26, 34, 103 |
| 25:20 | 61 |
| 25:26b | 22, 125 |
| 25:31 | 74 |
| 25:33 | 74 |
| 26:1–19 | 29, 40 |
| 26:3 | 61 |
| 26:7–11 | 26 |
| 26:9 | 61 |
| 26:12–15 | 26 |
| 26:17–19 | 3 |
| 26:20–23 | 38, 40 |
| 26:24 | 29, 40 |
| 27–28 | 26, 117 |
| 27 | 31 |
| 27:1–11 | 26 |
| 27:9 | 101 |
| 27:12–15 | 26 |
| 27:16–22 | 26 |
| 27:22 | 62 |
| 28 | 26, 32 |
| 29 | 30 |
| 29:2 | 8, 41 |
| 29:10–14 | 22 |
| 29:10 | 62 |
| 29:13 | 53 |
| 29:19 | 68 |
| 29:29–32 | 26 |
| 30–33 | 28, 75 |
| 30:6 | 95, 103 |
| 30:7 | 51 |
| 30:8 | 87 |
| 30:11 | 113 |
| 30:12–13 | 104 |
| 30:18–21 | 28 |
| 31:1–20 | 62 |
| 31:2–14 | 28 |
| 31:3 | 85 |
| 31:16–20 | 28 |
| 31:21–22 | 30 |
| 31:23–40 | 33 |
| 31:31–34 | 33, 38, 74 |
| 31:38 | 48 |
| 32 | 26 |
| 32:6–15 | 34, 117 |
| 32:6–12 | 26 |
| 32:29 | 52 |
| 32:33 | 67, 68 |
| 32:40 | 33 |
| 32:41 | 75 |
| 33:1–26 | 33 |
| 33:10 | 68 |
| 34:1–7 | 26 |
| 34:8–22 | 32 |
| 34:22 | 61 |
| 35 | 26 |
| 35:1–11 | 26, 117 |
| 35:13 | 67 |
| 35:14 | 68 |
| 35:15 | 68 |
| 36 | 26 |
| 36:1–26 | 22 |
| 36:1–10 | 40 |
| 36:1–8 | 29 |
| 36:3 | 61 |
| 36:9–26 | 29 |
| 36:9 | 8, 40 |
| 36:11–19 | 40 |
| 36:19 | 29 |
| 36:20–26 | 40 |
| 36:27–32 | 29 |
| 36:30 | 41 |
| 37:1—38:28 | 32 |
| 37:3–11 | 26 |
| 37:3–10 | 37 |

| | | | |
|---|---|---|---|
| 37:3-8 | 26 | 46:24-26 | 102 |
| 37:11-21 | 32 | 46:26b | 34 |
| 37:12-16 | 26 | 47 | 8, 40 |
| 37:17-20 | 26 | 47:4 | 61 |
| 38:1-13 | 33 | 48:9 | 61 |
| 38:1-6 | 26 | 48:26 | 62 |
| 38:7-13 | 26 | 48:29-30 | 62 |
| 38:14-28 | 26 | 48:47 | 34 |
| 39:7 | 103 | 49:1 | 62 |
| 39:11-14 | 25, 26, 34 | 49:2 | 62 |
| 39:15-18 | 26, 33 | 49:4 | 68 |
| 39:18 | 34 | 49:6 | 34 |
| 40:1-6 | 25, 26, 34 | 49:11 | 34 |
| 40:1 | 103 | 49:16 | 124 |
| 40:2 | 48 | 49:17 | 104 |
| 40:7-12 | 34 | 49:18 | 62 |
| 40:13—41:3 | 34 | 49:22 | 103 |
| 41:1-3 | 25 | 49:39 | 34 |
| 41:16—43:7 | 34 | 50:1—51:58 | 22 |
| 41:17 | 38 | 50:5 | 33 |
| 42:1—43:7 | 38 | 50:13 | 63, 104 |
| 42:1-22 | 26 | 50:15 | 82 |
| 42:7 | 117 | 50:23 | 124 |
| 43-44 | 34 | 50:28 | 82 |
| 43:1-4 | 26 | 50:37 | 103 |
| 43:7 | 25 | 50:38b | 126 |
| 43:8—44:30 | 34 | 50:40 | 62 |
| 43:8-13 | 26, 117 | 51:2 | 95 |
| 44:1-25 | 26 | 51:6 | 82 |
| 44:6 | 84 | 51:7 | 124, 125 |
| 44:15-25 | 46 | 51:20-24 | 124 |
| 45 | 33 | 51:29 | 61 |
| 45:5 | 34 | 51:30 | 103 |
| 46-51 | 34 | 51:58b | 125 |
| 46:2 | 7, 40, 94 | 51:59-64 | 26 |
| 46:3-6 | 94 | | |
| 46:9 | 95 | | |

## Lamentations

| | |
|---|---|
| 46:9a | 101 |
| 46:10 | 53 |
| 46:11 | 104 |
| 46:19 | 61 |

| | |
|---|---|
| 1:2 | 102 |
| 1:7 | 102 |
| 1:8-9 | 101 |
| 1:9 | 102 |

## Scripture Index

### Lamentations (cont.)

| | |
|---|---|
| 1:16–17 | 102 |
| 1:17 | 101 |
| 1:21 | 102 |
| 2:11–12 | 103 |
| 2:15 | 63, 104 |
| 2:19 | 103 |
| 3:25–26 | 74, 117 |
| 4:21 | 103 |
| 4:21b | 125 |

### Ezekiel

| | |
|---|---|
| 3:17–21 | 117 |
| 5:6 | 67 |
| 7:19 | 55 |
| 7:26 | 68 |
| 13:3 | 123 |
| 13:18 | 123 |
| 14:4–7 | 45 |
| 16:36–39 | 101 |
| 21:28–32 | 62 |
| 22:14 | 75 |
| 22:25 [LXX] | 67 |
| 22:26 | 67–68 |
| 22:27 | 67 |
| 23:25 | 75 |
| 23:28 | 67 |
| 23:29 | 75 |
| 25:3–7 | 62 |
| 25:6 | 104 |
| 25:8–11 | 62 |
| 25:14 | 82 |
| 25:16 | 61 |
| 30:3 | 53 |
| 30:14–16 | 102 |
| 33:7 | 117 |
| 34:11–15 | 74 |
| 34:12 | 55 |
| 34:16 | 75 |
| 36:5–7 | 82 |
| 38:19–20 | 52 |
| 39:17 | 53 |
| 39:25 | 82 |
| 39:26 | 74 |

### Hosea

| | |
|---|---|
| 2:3a | 101 |
| 2:5a [Heb] | 101 |
| 2:10 | 101 |
| 2:12 [Heb] | 101 |
| 2:16–17 | 74 |
| 2:18–19 [Heb] | 74 |
| 4:1–3 | 52 |
| 4:3 | 52 |
| 4:6—5:1 | 67 |
| 4:7 | 125 |
| 6:5 | 68 |
| 7:13 | 123 |
| 7:15 | 84 |
| 8:4b | 124 |
| 9:8 | 117 |
| 9:12 | 123 |
| 10:5 | 52 |
| 10:14b | 102 |
| 13:15 | 83 |

### Joel

| | |
|---|---|
| 1:4 | 104 |
| 1:12 | 83 |
| 1:15 | 53 |
| 2:2 | 55 |
| 2:5 | 95, 101 |
| 2:6 | 95 |
| 2:7 | 95, 104 |
| 2:9 | 104 |
| 2:10 | 55 |
| 2:13 | 83 |
| 2:27 | 75 |
| 2:30–31 | 55 |
| 3:3 | 103 |
| 3:11–16 | 74 |

| | | | |
|---|---|---|---|
| 3:14 | 53 | 3:11 | 67 |
| 4:3 [Heb] | 103 | 4:1–4 | 62 |
| | | 4:4 | 74 |
| | | 4:6–7 | 75 |

## Amos

| | | 5:11 [Heb] | 101 |
|---|---|---|---|
| 1:2 | 61 | 5:12 | 101 |
| 1:13 | 62 | 6:8 | 61 |
| 1:14 | 55 | 6:15 | 55 |
| 2:2 | 55 | 7:1 | 123 |
| 2:14–16 | 55 | 7:4 | 117 |
| 2:14 | 94 | 7:7 | 117, 134 |
| 4:2 | 114 | 7:14 | 74 |
| 4:11 | 62 | | |
| 5:6–7 | 61 | | |

## Nahum

| 5:6 | 63 | | |
|---|---|---|---|
| 5:11 | 55 | 1:1–11 | 91 |
| 5:14 | 61 | 1:1–3 | 81 |
| 5:125b | 61 | 1:1 | 17, 117 |
| 5:18–20 | 51, 55 | 1:2–11 | 17, 79–80 |
| 5:18 | 123 | 1:2–9 | 80 |
| 6:1 | 123 | 1:2 | 11, 55, 79, 81 |
| 6:2 | 61 | | |
| 7:2 | 84 | 1:3 | 12, 79, 82 |
| 8:9 | 55 | 1:4 | 79, 81, 83 |
| 9:1 | 59 | 1:5 | 79 |
| 9:7 | 58, 61 | 1:5a | 95 |
| | | 1:6 | 12, 80, 81 |

## Obadiah

| | | 1:7 | 74, 80 |
|---|---|---|---|
| 4 | 124 | 1:8–9 | 81 |
| 15 | 53 | 1:8 | 80 |
| 19–20 | 62 | 1:9–11 | 81 |
| | | 1:9 | 80 |
| | | 1:10 | 80 |

## Micah

| | | 1:11 | 80, 87, 91 |
|---|---|---|---|
| 1:4 | 83 | 1:12–14 | 17, 80, 86 |
| 2:1 | 123 | 1:12–13 | 87 |
| 2:2 | 67 | 1:12 | 80, 86 |
| 2:11 | 67 | 1:13 | 86 |
| 2:12 | 74 | 1:14 | 86, 88, 91 |
| 3:1–3 | 67 | 1:15—2:13 | 17, 89–91 |
| 3:6–7 | 67 | 1:15 | 17, 80, 87, 89, 91, 92 |
| 3:9–12 | 124–25 | | |

## Nahum (*cont.*)

| | |
|---|---|
| 2:1–15 [Heb] | 91 |
| 2:1–14 [Heb] | 89 |
| 2:1 [Heb] | 87, 89, 91, 92 |
| 2:2 [Heb] | 89–90, 89 |
| 2:3 [Heb] | 89–90 |
| 2:3 | 90 |
| 2:4 [Heb] | 90 |
| 2:4 | 90, 101 |
| 2:5 [Heb] | 90 |
| 2:5 | 90 |
| 2:6 [Heb] | 90 |
| 2:6 | 90 |
| 2:7 [Heb] | 90 |
| 2:7 | 90 |
| 2:8 [Heb] | 90 |
| 2:8 | 82, 90, 93 |
| 2:9 [Heb] | 90 |
| 2:9 | 90, 102 |
| 2:10 [Heb] | 90, 102 |
| 2:10 | 90, 93 |
| 2:11–12 | 101 |
| 2:11 [Heb] | 90 |
| 2:11 | 90, 93 |
| 2:12 [Heb] | 90 |
| 2:12 | 91 |
| 2:13 [Heb] | 91 |
| 2:13 | 60, 91, 100, 101 |
| 2:13b | 92 |
| 2:14 [Heb] | 60, 91 |
| 3:1–19 | 18, 97–99 |
| 3:1–4 | 100 |
| 3:1 | 91, 95, 96, 97, 99, 100, 123 |
| 3:2–3 | 101 |
| 3:2 | 97 |
| 3:3 | 97, 102 |
| 3:4 | 97 |
| 3:5–7 | 100, 101 |
| 3:5 | 60, 97–98, 100 |
| 3:5b | 125 |
| 3:6 | 98 |
| 3:7 | 59, 98 |
| 3:8–19 | 100 |
| 3:8 | 98, 102 |
| 3:9 | 98 |
| 3:10–11 | 100 |
| 3:10 | 98 |
| 3:11 | 98 |
| 3:12 | 98–99 |
| 3:13 | 99 |
| 3:14 | 99 |
| 3:15 | 99 |
| 3:16 | 99 |
| 3:17 | 99 |
| 3:18 | 99 |
| 3:19 | 63, 92, 99, 100 |
| 3:19b | 101 |

## Habakkuk

| | |
|---|---|
| 1:2–17 | 109–11 |
| 1:2–4 | 23, 24, 111, 114 |
| 1:2 | 20, 23, 109, 111 |
| 1:3 | 109 |
| 1:4 | 67, 109, 113 |
| 1:5–11 | 21, 23, 111 |
| 1:5 | 109, 112 |
| 1:6 | 109–10 |
| 1:7 | 110 |
| 1:8 | 110 |
| 1:9 | 110 |
| 1:10 | 110, 112 |
| 1:11 | 110 |

## Scripture Index

| | | | |
|---|---|---|---|
| 1:12—2:5 | 21 | 2:12 | 121, 123 |
| 1:12–17 | 23, 111 | 2:13 | 121 |
| 1:12–17 | 23, 111 | 2:14 | 121, 122 |
| 1:12 | 110 | 2:15 | 121, 123 |
| 1:13–17 | 117 | 2:16 | 121, 122 |
| 1:13 | 110 | 2:17 | 121, 122 |
| 1:14 | 110–11 | 2:18 | 121, 122, 123, 126 |
| 1:15 | 111, 112 | | |
| 1:16 | 111, 112 | 2:19 | 121–22, 122 |
| 1:17 | 111, 112, 116, 118 | 2:20 | 53, 122 |
| 2 | 21 | 3 | 23, 25, 117 |
| 2:1–5 | 115–16 | | |
| 2:1 | 23, 115, 116 | 3:1 | 130 |
| | | 3:2–19 | 128–30 |
| 2:2–5 | 23, 116 | 3:2 | 12, 128, 131, 134 |
| 2:2–4 | 21 | | |
| 2:2 | 115 | 3:3–15 | 117, 131, 135 |
| 2:3 | 23, 74, 115, 131, 134 | | |
| | | 3:3 | 128 |
| | | 3:4 | 128 |
| 2:4–5 | 118, 122 | 3:5 | 128 |
| 2:4 | 115–16, 118, 131 | 3:6 | 83, 128–29 |
| 2:5 | 116 | 3:7 | 129 |
| 2:5b | 118 | 3:8 | 129 |
| 2:6–20 | 21, 131 | 3:9 | 129, 133 |
| 2:6–19 | 118 | 3:10 | 83, 129 |
| 2:6 | 13, 123 | 3:11 | 129 |
| 2:6a | 116, 122 | 3:12 | 129 |
| 2:6b–20 | 23, 101, 120–22 | 3:13 | 129 |
| | | 3:14 | 129 |
| 2:6b | 120 | 3:15 | 129 |
| 2:7–8 | 122 | 3:16–19 | 131 |
| 2:7 | 120 | 3:16 | 23, 129 |
| 2:8 | 120, 122, 126 | 3:16b | 117 |
| | | 3:17–19 | 131 |
| 2:9 | 13, 120–21, 123 | 3:17 | 129–30 |
| | | 3:18 | 130 |
| 2:10 | 121, 122 | 3:19 | 130 |
| 2:11–12 | 13 | 3:19b | 130 |
| 2:11 | 121, 122 | | |

## Scripture Index

### Zephaniah

| Reference | Pages |
|---|---|
| 1:1 | 13 |
| 1:2–18 | 15 |
| 1:2–6 | 49 |
| 1:2–5 | 49 |
| 1:2 | 45, 60 |
| 1:3 | 45, 60 |
| 1:4–6 | 14 |
| 1:4 | 45 |
| 1:5 | 46 |
| 1:6 | 46, 68 |
| 1:7 | 46, 50, 53, 55, 126 |
| 1:8–11 | 50 |
| 1:8–10 | 49 |
| 1:8–9 | 14 |
| 1:8 | 4, 46 |
| 1:9 | 46, 48 |
| 1:10 | 46–47, 60 |
| 1:11 | 47 |
| 1:12–18 | 45–48, 50 |
| 1:12 | 4, 14, 47, 50 |
| 1:13 | 47, 55 |
| 1:14–16 | 50 |
| 1:14 | 47 |
| 1:15 | 47–48, 50 |
| 1:16 | 48 |
| 1:17 | 48, 50 |
| 1:18 | 48 |
| 2:1–15 | 52, 57–59 |
| 2:1–4 | 15, 59, 60 |
| 2:1 | 57, 59, 60 |
| 2:2 | 57, 60 |
| 2:3 | 14, 57, 60, 74 |
| 2:4–15 | 14, 60 |
| 2:4 | 57, 59, 60 |
| 2:5–15 | 15 |
| 2:5 | 58, 60, 123 |
| 2:6–7 | 60 |
| 2:6 | 58 |
| 2:7 | 14, 58 |
| 2:8–9 | 60, 62 |
| 2:8 | 58 |
| 2:9 | 58, 60 |
| 2:10–11 | 62 |
| 2:10 | 58, 59 |
| 2:11–12 | 60 |
| 2:11 | 58, 74 |
| 2:12 | 59, 60, 62 |
| 2:13–15 | 15, 20, 60, 62 |
| 2:13 | 59 |
| 2:14 | 59 |
| 2:15 | 59 |
| 3:1–7 | 16, 65–66, 66 |
| 3:1–5 | 66 |
| 3:1 | 65, 66, 123 |
| 3:2 | 14, 65 |
| 3:3–4 | 14, 112 |
| 3:3 | 65, 66, 113 |
| 3:4 | 65 |
| 3:5 | 65–66, 66 |
| 3:6–7 | 66 |
| 3:6 | 48, 66, 67 |
| 3:7 | 66 |
| 3:8–20 | 70–72 |
| 3:8–13 | 72 |
| 3:8 | 60, 66, 70, 72 |
| 3:9 | 70, 72 |
| 3:10 | 70 |
| 3:11 | 14, 70–71, 73 |
| 3:12 | 14, 71, 73 |
| 3:13 | 14, 71, 72, 73 |

## Scripture Index

| | |
|---|---|
| 3:14–17 | 14, 72 |
| 3:14 | 71, 74 |
| 3:15 | 71, 73 |
| 3:16 | 71, 73 |
| 3:17 | 71, 73 |
| 3:18–20 | 72 |
| 3:18 | 71, 75 |
| 3:19 | 72, 73 |
| 3:20 | 60, 72, 73 |

### Zechariah

| | |
|---|---|
| 2:13 | 53 |
| 2:17 [Heb] | 53 |

## APOCRYPHA

### Wisdom of Solomon

| | |
|---|---|
| 13:15–16 | 126 |

### Sirach

| | |
|---|---|
| 49:10 | 10 |

## NEW TESTAMENT

### Matthew

| | |
|---|---|
| 7:7–11 | 63 |
| 10:15 | 62 |
| 11:20–24 | 56 |
| 11:29 | 88 |
| 23:13–36 | 123 |
| 24:1–51 | 56 |

### Luke

| | |
|---|---|
| 15:7 | 76 |

### Romans

| | |
|---|---|
| 1:17 | 116, 118 |
| 2:4–11 | 134 |
| 5:1 | 116 |
| 8:25 | 76 |

### 1 Corinthians

| | |
|---|---|
| 12:2 | 126 |

### Galatians

| | |
|---|---|
| 3:11 | 116, 118 |

### 1 Thessalonians

| | |
|---|---|
| 5:1–10 | 56 |

### 2 Thessalonians

| | |
|---|---|
| 2:1–12 | 56 |

### Hebrews

| | |
|---|---|
| 6:13 | 62 |
| 10:37–39 | 116, 118 |

### 2 Peter

| | |
|---|---|
| 3:1–13 | 56 |
| 2:6 | 62 |

### Revelation

| | |
|---|---|
| 9:9 | 101 |

www.ingramcontent.com/pod-product-compliance
Lightning Source LLC
Chambersburg PA
CBHW022114160426
43197CB00009B/1026